D1112902

Spike Lee

Also by Jim Haskins

BILL COSBY: AMERICA'S MOST FAMOUS FATHER?

OUTWARD DREAMS: BLACK INVENTORS AND

THEIR INVENTIONS

AGAINST ALL OPPOSITION: BLACK EXPLORERS

IN AMERICA

FROM AFAR TO ZULU: A DICTIONARY OF

AFRICAN TRIBES

LOUIS FARRAKHAN AND THE NATION OF ISLAM

Walker and Company/New York

Spík

BY ANY MEA

Jim Haskins

e Lee

NECESSARY

First published in the United States of America in 1997 by Walker Publishing Company, Inc.

Published simultaneously in Canada by Thomas Allen & Son Canada,
Limited, Markham, Ontario

Library of Congress Cataloging-in-Publication Data
Haskins, James, 1941–
Spike Lee: by any means necessary/Jim Haskins.
p.   cm.
Includes bibliographical references and index.
Summary: Examines the life and works of the filmmaker who has
chosen to explore the many dimensions of the black American
experience.
ISBN 0-8027-8494-1 (hardcover). —ISBN 0-8027-8496-8 (reinforced)
1. Lee, Spike—Juvenile literature.   2. Motion picture producers
and directors—United States—Biography—Juvenile literature.
3. Afro-American motion picture producers and directors—United
States—Biography—Juvenile literature.   [1. Lee, Spike.   2. Motion
picture producers and directors.   3. Afro-Americans—Biography.]
I. Title.
PN1998.3.L44H38   1997
791.43′0233′092—dc20
[B]   96-41774
CIP
AC

Book design by Jennifer Ann Daddio

Printed in the United States of America

2   4   6   8   10   9   7   5   3   1

To Robert Hairston

I am grateful to Kathy Benson,

Deidre Grafel, and Ann Kalkhoff

for their help.

Contents

Spike Lee

1

Little Guy

As the winter of 1991–92 set in, all the footage for *Malcolm X*, Spike Lee's film biography of the charismatic black leader who was assassinated in 1965, had been shot. Ahead lay the postproduction phase of filmmaking, the job of editing the thousands of feet of celluloid into a motion picture. This was going to be an epic film, Lee had decided, at least three hours long. But that meant lots of money. By January he was $5,000 over his budget of $28 million. He wanted more money. But the Completion Bond Company, which insures investors against films going over budget, took financial control of the film and informed Lee that his film was to be no longer than two hours and fifteen minutes, although he could keep control of the editing.

Lee reinvested $2 million of his $3 million salary, but that was still not enough. So he did something unprecedented in Hollywood. He got on the telephone and asked wealthy blacks in the entertainment business to give him the money he needed to get his film made the way he wanted it. He emphasized that he was not asking for an investment, nor for a loan, but for an *outright gift*.

Spike Lee

The first person he called was Bill Cosby. A check was delivered to Lee's Los Angeles hotel that same day. Oprah Winfrey gave money. So did Magic Johnson, Michael Jordan, Prince, Janet Jackson, and Peggy Cooper-Cafritz, founder of the Duke Ellington School of the Arts in Washington, D.C. They all understood what Spike Lee represented in the world of filmmaking: He was a trailblazer, a black man who had managed to make Hollywood films his own way. Like other blacks in the United States, he had been forced to be twice as good to get half as far, to function as a spokesperson for the entire race when he was really only interested in speaking for himself, to be all things to all black people and at the same time not anger whites. So they gave him the money, no strings attached, and he made his film. It was his proudest achievement—a big-budget, epic film that introduced Malcolm X to a whole new generation of people, black and white, and made him a hero for the 1990s.

When he was alive, Malcolm X would say that black people should seize equal rights by "any means necessary." That phrase, which Spike Lee had read in *The Autobiography of Malcolm X* in junior high school, had stayed with him. He had applied it to his determination to make realistic films about black people. He had refused to give up. A fierce competitor all his life, he had taken on Hollywood and had become a major player.

Spike Lee was born Shelton Jackson Lee on March 20, 1957, in Atlanta, Georgia. A small, wiry little boy, he was soon nicknamed Spike by his mother. His mother, Jacquelyn, was a schoolteacher. His father, Bill, was a jazz composer and bass player. Both his parents were college educated. His father had attended the all-black Morehouse College in Atlanta. When Bill Lee arrived at Morehouse as a freshman, Martin Luther King, Jr., the future great civil rights leader, was a senior.

In the early 1950s, when Bill and Jacquelyn met and married, it was unusual for both the husband and wife in a black family to have college degrees. But the Lees were an even more unusual couple, for three of their parents also had college degrees. Still more remarkable was that one of their grandfathers was also college educated.

Spike was born only three years after the U.S. Supreme Court had ruled against segregated education. Until that time, all schools in the South, and some schools in the border states as well, had provided what they called "separate but equal" schools for whites and blacks. But the schools for blacks had never been equal. Classes were usually held in unheated churches or rundown buildings, teachers were not paid as much as white teachers, and books and other school supplies were castoffs from the white schools. The white children who lived far away from their schools could ride school buses. There were no school buses for black children, no matter how far away they lived from their schools. For white children, the school year was nine months long; for black children, it was only five months, so they could work in the fields during planting and harvesting time. Most black youngsters never graduated from high school, and only a very few ever made it to college. The proud history of college education in the Lee family placed them in the tiny southern black middle class, although economically they were hardly comfortable.

Since Bill Lee made his living as a musician, he did not earn a steady income. He and his wife had a "commuter marriage" at the time of Spike's birth. Jacquelyn lived in Atlanta with her parents. Bill spent most of his time in Chicago, playing with various bands and some of the top singers of the day, including Billie Holiday, Carmen McRae, and Sarah Vaughan. For the first year or so, Bill Lee saw his baby son only on infrequent weekends.

With Bill Lee away in Chicago, Spike was very much the center of Jacquelyn Lee's world. She kept him so close to her that her own mother, Zimmie Shelton, worried that she was overprotecting little Spike. She used to tell her daughter, "Let Spikey go, he's just a little kid now."[1] She didn't want her first grandchild to be a "Mama's boy."

But there was little danger of that. Spike Lee was tough from the start.

By the time Spike was a year old, Jacquelyn Lee had taken him to join Bill in Chicago. Their second son, Chris, was born there in 1959. But they did not remain in Chicago long. Many of Bill Lee's musician friends in Chicago were moving to New York, and he was beginning to feel left behind. In 1959, when Spike was two years old and Chris just an infant, the Lee family relocated to New York City.

They settled first in the Crown Heights section of Brooklyn, where American blacks and West Indian blacks lived uneasily with the predominantly Hasidic Jewish population. From there, they moved to 186 Warren Street in the Cobble Hill section of Brooklyn, the first neighborhood Spike Lee can actually remember living in. At that time Cobble Hill was predominantly Italian. In fact, according to Spike, the Lees were the first black family to move into the area. He was much too young to understand what that meant, and when he talks now about arriving in New York, he is retelling stories his parents told him. "For the first couple of days, we got called 'nigger,' but we were basically left alone," he has said. "We weren't perceived as a threat, because there was only one of us."[2]

Among Spike's best friends in Cobble Hill were the Tucci brothers, Louis and Joe. He does not recall having any problems because he was black and they were Italian. They were all little kids who were not old enough to be concerned about race. Even later, after he became aware of racial differences, Spike does not remember experiencing racism in the neighborhood. He recalls that there were a lot of Jewish families in Cobble Hill and that the neighborhood was quite tolerant.

Still, he wasn't completely insulated from racism. It still pains him to remember the time he tried to join the Cub Scouts: "All my friends were Cub Scouts. They'd go away camping, learn how to tie knots, do secret handshakes and stuff, wear them uniforms."[3] So he went to St. Peter's Church on Court Street to join up, only to be told that you had to be Catholic to be a Cub Scout. That wasn't true, of course; but it was a way to keep him out.

New York was a jazz city, and Bill Lee found work with bands in various clubs and, later, as a studio musician. One of Spike's earliest memories of his father is seeing the older man, who was small like his son, lugging around his big bass. By the early 1960s, Bill and Jacquelyn Lee felt secure enough financially to further increase their family. David was born two years after Chris. Joy (the only girl) was born a year after David. Cinque, born four years after Joy, was the fifth and last child and was named after the slave who led a successful slave revolt on the Spanish ship *Amistad* in 1839.

"I grew up the oldest," Spike Lee once commented, "so I had to be practical. The oldest child has to take care of the younger kids. They're always the most practical."⁴ When the family fell on hard times, Spike was the only one old enough to understand. By the middle 1960s Bill Lee was not getting as much work as before. More and more jazz bands wanted electric bass players, and Bill Lee refused to adapt to the new style. He had no use for the Fender bass. He wouldn't compromise his art, and as a consequence, he got less and less work. Jacquelyn Lee got a teaching job to help out, and more often than not, the family lived on her salary.

The Lees were not so poor that they were forced to give up their home, but there were times when their telephone service was cut off because they could not pay the bill. They never missed a meal, but sometimes the food on the table was very skimpy.

Still, Bill and Jacquelyn Lee made sure their children never lacked what they considered the important things in life. As soon as the children could understand, they were taught to be proud of their family and to appreciate their roots. Every summer they piled into the family car and drove down South to visit each set of grandparents. Spike remembers spending half the summer with his maternal grandparents in Atlanta and half with his father's family in Snow Hill, Alabama, near Selma.

The trips took more than twenty hours, and even after segregation was legally ended in 1964, the Lees did not feel comfortable stopping at previously segregated roadside restaurants or service station restrooms. The children grew restless and fought among themselves, and the Lee parents yelled from the front seat. But they believed the trips were worth the trouble to give the children a strong sense of family and their roots.

Spike remembers seeing separate restrooms for whites and "colored" in the South when he was small. But seeing segregation at work had less of an effect on him than experiencing the strong faith and sense of history of his grandparents. Spike and his brothers and sister dressed up in their best and attended church every Sunday, ate a formal Sunday dinner afterward, and listened to the family traditions the grandparents wanted to pass down.

Spike was proud of his grandparents' and one great-grandfather's college education. But he was even more impressed with a story from his father's family that went back to slave times. It was about two slaves named Mike and Phoebe who belonged to different masters in South Carolina.

They fell in love and were married on Christmas Day 1811. They had seven children, and Phoebe was pregnant with their eighth when her owner decided to move to Alabama. Since he owned Phoebe, and thus her children, he planned to take them all with him. Mike was distraught at the prospect of losing his family. He begged to be sold to Phoebe's owner, but his request was denied.

He then asked to buy his freedom. His owner agreed—for $1,900, a fortune in those days. Mike worked for years to save that much money. He managed to do so, bought his freedom, and then set off for Alabama in search of his family. In May 1825 he was reunited with Phoebe in Snow Hill, Alabama. They remained together—he free, she enslaved—for forty years and had three more children. Phoebe died a year before the South surrendered to the North and Alabama's slaves were freed. She and Mike were Spike Lee's great-great-grandparents.

On his mother's side of the family, Spike learned about black pride from his grandmother, Zimmie Shelton. Even when Spike's mother was young, Zimmie insisted that she have black dolls. In those days there were few commercially made black dolls, and Zimmie Shelton thought those that were available were ugly. But she preferred an ugly black doll to a white one. Greeting cards and children's books had only white children's pictures in them. So Zimmie sat down at her kitchen table and put a thin wash of brown watercolor over the white faces to make them brown. She refused to give her daughter a birthday card with a white child's face on it, and she would not read her daughter a book in which all the characters were white. She was a strong believer in education and impressed upon her grandchildren the importance of getting as much schooling as they could.

The same fall that Spike's mother walked him to Public School 29 to start kindergarten, blacks in the South were still fighting for an equal education. In Mississippi, at the state university everyone called Ole Miss, James Meredith, a young black Mississippian, was escorted by federal troops to register at the previously all-white school. In New York City, Spike and his sister and brothers did not have to face that kind of discrimination, and they knew they were lucky. Also enviable was Spike's strong sense of family history. As his friend Monty Ross, who met Spike at Morehouse College in 1975, puts it, "To know your lines, those generations—to have *history* . . . that's a very powerful thing."[5]

Partly because he was the oldest child in his family, and partly because of his own nature, Spike was not just a leader in the Lee family but also a leader among neighborhood kids. He was very quiet. (His grandmother Zimmie thought he was *too* quiet.) But when he did speak, the other kids listened. He was the organizer, whether it was a game of softball or a trip to the local pool. He got into his share of trouble, but it was just kid mischief, not anything serious. In those days it was very hard for a child to get into trouble because every adult in the neighborhood watched the children and made sure they behaved. If someone else's mother saw you doing something wrong, she would lecture you as if you were her own child—and then tell your mother what you had done.

No drug pushers would have been allowed to hang around. No gangs would have been allowed to form. Some of the bigger guys in the neighborhood preyed on the younger kids, making them give up their lunch money, but that was the extent of the neighborhood crime. Spike was the kind of scrawny, small kid who was easy prey, and he was practical, so he just gave up his quarters and borrowed from a friend to buy lunch. Today, he cannot imagine what it must be like to grow up amid the violence and fear that plague so many inner-city neighborhoods.

This sense of safety was found in all the Brooklyn neighborhoods where Spike grew up. In 1968, after Bill Lee started working as a musician with folk singers, the family was doing well enough to buy a brownstone house in Brooklyn's Fort Greene section. Number 165 Washington Park faced the park of the same name. It was across the street from a housing project, but the housing project was not the crime-ridden, drug-infested type of housing project that we so often hear about today. The families who lived in the project worked hard, and Spike Lee does not remember looking down on the project kids because they were not as well off as he and his family.

In grade school and junior high, Spike was an above-average student who hated math and science but enjoyed social studies. His mother always thought he could do better. She knew him well enough to understand that he was just doing enough to get by, and she was constantly nagging him to study more. But Spike did not find much that interested him at school, and he refused to study harder just because his mother wanted him to.

Much of Spike's education came outside of school. By the time Cinque was born, many black Americans had grown tired of the struggle for integration. Having experienced, or watched on television, the violent reaction with which southern white racists greeted the nonviolent civil rights movement's attempts to win equality, they had turned away from integration and to an emphasis on black nationalism. Black, or cultural, nationalism stressed pride in the African roots of black Americans. Jacquelyn Lee was inspired to emphasize her family's African heritage, and she taught her children to be proud of it. She wore her hair in cornrows and did little Joy's hair the same way—complete with cowrie shell beads—long before it became generally fashionable among blacks to do so. The name she gave her youngest child, Cinque, also attested to her pride in her African heritage.

When Spike and the other children were old enough, their mother gave them books to read by black writers like Langston Hughes, for in those days there was no Black History Month or multicultural curriculum, and she knew she could not rely on the local public schools to teach her children about their own history. Jacquelyn Lee loved literature and art. She took Spike and his siblings to plays and museums.

Bill Lee saw to his children's musical education. Every single one of them took music lessons. Spike learned piano and violin at home and learned to play the recorder at school along with his classmates, but he never took to any of these instruments. He says that this was part of his rebelliousness as the oldest child. His brothers and his sister liked playing music, so there was always someone practicing in the house. Bill Lee sometimes took Spike with him to the Blue Note and other Manhattan jazz clubs where he played. After his refusal to adapt to the electric bass made his jazz jobs few and far between, he turned increasingly to folk music, which had not yet gone electric. He recorded many folk albums and often accompanied folk singers in live performances. Every summer, in addition to their regular trip South, the whole family piled into their station wagon and headed for the Newport Folk Festival in Newport, Rhode Island, where Bill Lee played with folk singers like Josh White and Odetta; Joan Baez and Peter, Paul, and Mary; Bob Dylan and Pete Seeger.

As children, Spike and his brothers and sister went to a lot of movies. Spike can remember his mother taking him to see the film *Bye Bye Birdie* at Radio City Music Hall, as well as to James Bond movies like *Goldfinger* and *Dr. No* and the Beatles movie *A Hard Day's Night.* The first movie that made a big impression on him was *Hatari!,* a film about a safari starring John Wayne, because he was intrigued by the rhinoceros.

The great majority of these movies starred whites, like John Wayne and Sean Connery (who played the lead in the James Bond films). When Spike was growing up, very few black actors were offered starring or even major roles. The one exception was Sidney Poitier, but the parts in which he was cast were not very realistic.

Spike remembers that he was only about six or seven when he saw his first Sidney Poitier movie, *Lilies of the Field.* In it, Poitier plays a drifter who is hired as a handyman by a group of nuns and who ends up building a church for them. "I hated that movie," Lee once said. "I felt like putting a rock through the screen. Later with these nuns!"[6] He didn't believe that anybody would be as nice as that handyman. Even then, young Spike understood in some way that "the only way they [white audiences] could accept this guy was because he was a perfect human being."[7]

Spike continued to see a lot of movies when he was old enough to go alone or with his friends. But so did all the other kids in the neighborhood. Movie making held no special interest for Spike. "I had no idea that people made movies," he wrote in his book *Five for Five*. "I just didn't know. You went to the movie house, the lights went out, the movie came on, you enjoyed it, you ate as much popcorn and candy as you could eat, you drank as much Coke as you could drink, the movie ended, the lights came on, and you [went home]. Movies were magic—and something you couldn't do. Or so you thought."[8]

What interested Spike Lee most as a youngster was sports—all sports, from basketball, to football, to baseball. Although he was not the best athlete, he was always captain of the team, because he was very competitive. Spike Lee liked to win. When he wasn't playing, he was watching sports on TV and during the New York Knicks' season was constantly fighting with his sister over whether to watch the Knicks' games or *The Brady Bunch*.

In 1968, when he was eleven, Lee began riding the subway from Brooklyn to Madison Square Garden. Back then, the best seats he could afford were high above the basketball court. His hero was the shooting guard Walt Frazier, with his cool, unflappable attitude and dead-sure shot. Once, Frazier dropped by the Manhattan club where Bill Lee was playing. For young Spike Lee, it was the thrill of a lifetime.

Baseball was actually his favorite sport, and until he was in high school he determined to be a baseball player when he grew up.

From an early age he collected baseball cards and other memorabilia. He also collected the autographs of his favorite players. He spent a lot of time hanging around outside ballparks and hotels waiting for a chance to shove a piece of paper in front of a player, often to be disappointed by a man who was too tired or too busy to stop and sign his name. It seemed to Lee that the least a player could do was take a little time for a fan who spent his every waking hour thinking about baseball. When he became famous himself, he made a point of signing autographs for kids.

Spike and Chris, the brother closest to him in age, both went to public elementary and junior high schools. By the time the next brother, David, was ready to enter school, Jacquelyn Lee had gotten a job teaching literature and art at St. Ann's, a Catholic school in Brooklyn Heights, which included all grades from primary through high school. She was the first black teacher to be hired at the school, and she later introduced the first black history course there. Her position as a teacher at St. Ann's allowed her to enroll her children at a reduced tuition, and so the youngest three Lee children—David, Joy, and Cinque—all went to St. Ann's.

Spike and Chris could have attended St. Ann's as well, but they had experienced racism and did not want to go to a virtually all-white school. Spike does not regret not having attended private school. In fact, he believes he received a better education in life by attending public school. "I always could tell a difference in them [his younger siblings] because they went to private school," he once said. "Their negritude got honed or harnessed going into these predominantly white private schools."[9]

When it came time to choose a high school, Spike applied to and was accepted at John Dewey High School, which had higher academic standards and offered a more varied curriculum than the public high schools that were closer to his home. Located in Coney Island, it had an ethnically mixed student body. There were enough black students to make Spike feel comfortable and enough white students to give him the opportunity to get to know people who were different from him.

Some of his friends had very unpleasant high school experiences. Academically unprepared for a high school like John Dewey, they attended Fort Hamilton High and Franklin Delano Roosevelt High. These schools were located in predominantly white neighborhoods, and a lot of Spike's friends were regularly chased from the school to the subway station. Even though he himself did not have racial run-ins, hearing his friends talk about theirs caused Spike to be attuned to and resentful of white racism. That was what he meant when he spoke of his younger brothers and sisters and their "negritude." His was better honed, he believes; he was more sensitive to racial slights than they were.

In fact, he was sensitive to life in general. Shy, he had very few close friends, although he was generally well liked. He was embarrassed by his small size. At the time, large Afro hairstyles were in vogue, and Spike wore a huge one, which added a good three or four inches to his height. If he was interested in a girl, he was too self-conscious about his size to risk approaching her and then being rebuffed. He was more interested in playing stickball than in dating.

By the time he reached high school, Spike Lee had accepted the fact that he was going to be small like his father. He wasn't going to grow tall enough or big enough to be able to compete in sports. At full growth, Spike would be only five feet, six inches tall and 120 pounds. A career as an athlete was definitely out.

Spike Lee was going to be a little guy. That knowledge bothered him for a while. But he was practical. He decided that he would be important in some other way. He just didn't know what way. His father once remarked that Spike was so little he just had to do something big.

2

College Man

There had never been any question that Spike would go to college. It was part of the family tradition. He never even thought about rebelling by not going to college. And when the time came to choose a school, there was little question that he would attend Morehouse, where his father and grandfather had gone before him. Spike looked forward to carrying on the family tradition. He also looked forward to going to a school where the student body and the faculty were predominantly black.

Having spent so many summers with his grandparents in Atlanta, Spike felt comfortable in the city. But the world of the Atlanta University complex was new to him. Surrounded by so many examples of black excellence, he was impressed when he entered Morehouse in the fall of 1975. But later he began to feel alienated.

He thought the food was terrible, so he ate many of his meals at his grandmother Zimmie Shelton's house, riding his bicycle the four blocks from the school at least once, and frequently twice, a day. At first, his primary mission was to fill his stomach, but as time went on he escaped to his grandmother's because he did not feel comfortable at Morehouse.

He found what he considered a very distinct class separation based primarily on skin color and hair texture. As he would later say, "The people with the money, most of them have light skin. They have the Porsches, the BMW's, the quote good hair unquote. The others, the kids from the rural South, have bad, kinky hair. When I was in school, we saw all this going on. I remember saying, 'Some of this stuff has to be in a movie.' "[1]

Skin color and hair texture aside, there seemed to be a very conventional, middle-class mold one was supposed to fit into, and Spike did not fit. The "Morehouse Man" was tall, light complected, and good looking, drove a nice car, dressed like a model, and had his pick of the girls. Spike Lee, at eighteen, looked about thirteen. With his skinny legs, bushy Afro hairstyle, and big glasses, he was about as far from the ideal Morehouse Man as he could be. Instead of driving a car of any kind, he rode a bicycle. His idea of dressing up was to exchange his shorts for long pants and to put on a clean T-shirt. He didn't even try to ask a girl out on a date, certain that if he did he would be refused.

Anyway, he did not want to fit the mold of the Morehouse Man. Or at least that's what he told himself. He did not openly rebel, but he went his own way and began to feel stifled by an environment that did not seem to allow for differences. To him, it seemed as if the administration and faculty were still trying to impress whites, just as they had years earlier, when the faculty and board of trustees had been predominantly white. Though the governing authorities at the college were now almost all black, Spike came to the conclusion that Morehouse and Spelman, its sister school, were "very backward."

Homesick, he called his mother frequently and wrote her long letters—which she sent back with his grammar and spelling corrected in red ink. Spike never got the opportunity to work out his relationship with the school and the image it wanted its students to project, for soon these influences gave way to ones closer to home.

In his sophomore year, Spike learned that his mother had liver cancer. It was an especially quick-moving cancer, and before he could even adjust to the fact that his mother was ill, she was dead. Only nineteen when Jacquelyn Lee died on October 28, 1976, Spike found it very hard to accept his mother's death. But he felt it was his responsibility to help his younger brothers and sister—Joy was only fourteen—to handle the same pain he himself was feeling.

"I didn't even cry at my mother's funeral," he wrote in his book *Five for Five*. "I wanted to, but I felt I couldn't let my younger brothers and sister see me break down and do that. I had to be strong. Now, I'm not equating tears with weakness, but I believed at the time that because I was the eldest, my brothers and sister were looking to me for strength."[2] He kept much of his pain and sense of loss to himself. He was planning somehow to make his mark on the world. But now, his mother would not be around to see it, and she was the one he wanted most to please.

By his junior year, Spike had satisfied the basic liberal arts course requirements at Morehouse and was able to choose more specialized courses. He majored in mass communications and took courses in journalism as well as radio and television. He wrote articles for the school newspaper and had his own radio show on WCLK, a jazz station at nearby Clark College. He really had no idea what he wanted to do or what field he would one day choose. But Spike believed he would eventually find out what he wanted to do after he got practical experience in a variety of fields.

Spike Lee continued to go to lots of movies while at Morehouse, and it was a natural next step for him to buy a video camera. After his sophomore year, in the summer of 1977, he bought a super-8 video camera and noodled around taking footage of his family and friends. That same summer, a power failure blacked out large portions of the Northeast. In New York City, especially in the poorer neighborhoods, some people took advantage of the general confusion and went on a looting spree. Spike recorded looting in his Brooklyn neighborhood.

In his junior year, Spike went to see Michael Cimino's film *The Deer Hunter* with his friend John Wilson and some other students. When the film was over, they emerged from the theater into pouring rain, so they all piled into a cab back to campus. Interviewed years later, Wilson recalled that in the cab Spike turned to him and said, "John, I know what I want to do. I want to make films."[3]

From then on, he could talk of little else, and he gravitated toward people who were also interested in movies. That was how he and Monty Ross became friends. By the time they actually met through a mutual friend they were attending different schools, for Ross had transferred from Morehouse to Clark College, also a part of the Atlanta University system. But since they both wanted to make movies—Ross to act in them and Lee to direct them—they had something in common.

Zimmie Shelton had replaced Spike's mother as his emotional anchor. He called her Mama and visited her often. He and Monty

Ross used to sit on Zimmie's porch after she had cooked them dinner and talk about making movies.

Not long before, Hollywood had put out a lot of black films. After the huge success of independent filmmaker Melvin Van Peebles' *Sweet Sweetback's Baadasssss Song* in 1971, quite a number of black films were made, and some were not only critically acclaimed but also written and directed by blacks, such as Gordon Parks' *The Learning Tree*. These films had done so well at the box office, and especially among black audiences, that Hollywood studios had hurried to make more black movies. But while the actors and actresses in these quickly made films were black, the writers, producers, and directors were mostly white.

Most of the films that were rushed out to take advantage of the "new" black market were poorly written and filled with sex and gangster violence. Someone coined the term "blaxploitation" to describe films that were made merely to exploit the current interest in black movies. Audiences, both black and white, seemed to sense that they were being exploited and stopped going to these movies. By around 1976, three years before Spike graduated from Morehouse, Hollywood had ceased making many black films.

Those that were being made may have featured a few blacks, but there were mostly whites behind the cameras, writing the lines they spoke, directing them, and producing the films. At the time, there was one good black role model making films in Hollywood, and that was Richard Pryor, who had first achieved fame as a standup comedian. After he had proven he could attract audiences, black and white, to see him in films such as *Car Wash* and *Silver Streak* (both 1977), Pryor had worked hard to ensure that more blacks got work both behind and in front of the cameras on the films he starred in.

It was a major concern of Spike's that there were so few blacks in Hollywood working behind the cameras—as producers, directors, cinematographers. Spike wanted to change that situation. His friends remember that he was always scribbling in notebooks, making plans for movies, dreaming of ushering in a new era of black filmmaking in Hollywood. As John Wilson put it, "Spike didn't just want to get in the door of the house [Hollywood]. He wanted to get in, rearrange the furniture—then go back and publicize the password."[4]

Having a goal in life seemed to give Spike a confidence he had not known before at Morehouse. In his junior year, when he finally looked old enough to be in college rather than high school, he had started to get over his shyness with women and summoned up the courage to go on a few dates, although he had no serious relationships. In spite of not fitting into the Morehouse Man mold, he had won the respect of his classmates during his years at the school. When the time came to choose someone to organize the annual coronation pageant on homecoming weekend of his senior year, the practical, clear-thinking, well-organized Spike got the job.

The year before, he had assisted a friend on the coronation pageant, and he had definite ideas about what he wanted. Usually, the pageant was very much like a bathing suit contest, featuring the prettiest girls in skimpy outfits. But Spike felt it was more appropriate for the young women to be dressed in ball gowns. He wanted to present them as queens. He was criticized for this idea. The Morehouse Men were accustomed to seeing a lot of "skin" at their homecoming pageant, and a group even threatened to beat Spike up if he didn't give them what they wanted. But he stuck to his idea, and the pageant he produced was memorable for its beauty.

Spike shot a couple of movies while at Morehouse. He says now that they were forgettable, and they probably were. But they show the interests he would pursue in his more mature films. The 1977 *Black College: The Talented Tenth* starred his friend Monty Ross and Rolanda Watts, who was then attending Spelman and who later became a reporter on local television in New York and the host of a talk show. The film referred to an idea proposed in 1903 by the great African-American scholar W. E. B. Du Bois: that it was the duty of the most talented one-tenth of the black population to lead the other nine-tenths. But it was less an exploration of that notion than a love story that took place at an all-black college. Lee now considers it corny and refuses to allow it to be shown. In the 1978 film, *Last Hustle in Brooklyn*, Lee juxtaposed the footage he had taken of looting during the 1977 blackout with scenes of disco dancers.

These films were amateur attempts, and Lee knew that. He wanted to learn how to really make films, and in his senior year he applied to and was accepted at the film school at New York University. His grandmother Zimmie offered to pay his tuition, for with Jacquelyn Lee's death, money had become very tight in the Lee family. He was also accepted as a summer intern at Columbia Pictures in Burbank, California. He could have attended film school in California, and since the majority of movies are made on the West Coast, he briefly considered doing so. But Spike Lee didn't drive, which would have been an extreme handicap in Los Angeles, where the public transportation system is not extensive and where nothing is within walking distance of anything else. Also, he found out that at the West Coast film schools in which he was interested, not every student got to make films. A faculty committee chose those who were fortunate enough to make them. Moreover, one had to have high scores on the Graduate Record Exam, and Spike's were not high.

Lee decided against going to a California film school. Instead he would go home. Since his mother's death, he had felt a need to have family around him—and NYU was a fine school, a good choice professionally. Plus he knew New York, and he could get to wherever he wanted to go either on his bicycle or by bus or subway.

Spike graduated from Morehouse in the spring of 1979 and headed out to the West Coast for his internship in Hollywood. He did not learn much about filmmaking, but he did learn that making films was less an art than a business. It took money to make films, and success was measured by how much a film earned at the box office. Spike listened and took mental notes and would later apply what he had learned when he made his own films.

That there were few blacks in the movie business was something Spike already knew. But his summer in Hollywood confirmed his awareness that black faces were especially rare in the technical and creative areas.

Back at home in Brooklyn and facing two or three years living with his family while attending NYU, Spike found it difficult to adjust to a home without his mother. He spent as much time as he could with his younger brothers and sister and tried hard to make up for the loss of their mother. But in trying to be strong for them, he may have swallowed his own pain too deeply.

Further, a new element had been added to the family's emotional landscape. Bill Lee was dating a white, Jewish woman whom he had met in a club in Manhattan where he worked from time to time. After a while, Susan Kaplan moved in. It might have been hard for Spike to adjust to any new woman in his father's life, but a white woman was especially hard to take. His mother had been so proud of her blackness.

But Susan Kaplan's color was not the main sore point. What bothered Spike Lee was the insult to his mother's memory. Of all the Lee children, Spike was the most adamant in his refusal to accept Susan Kaplan, whom his father later married, and the resulting family dissension caused him to feel that he had lost not only his mother but the rest of his family as well. He continued to resent the situation for years. In 1992 he said of Susan Kaplan, "She's good for my father, but at the expense of the entire family. Everybody has to seek their own happiness. He's happy now. But the cohesion of the family was destroyed. Any stepmother must realize that when you come into a family, you're an outsider, a stranger. Come with some humility. She came like gangbusters. My mother wasn't even cold in the grave."[5] Spike determined to leave home as soon as he was able. Until that time, he plunged himself into his film studies.

The New York University Institute of Film and Television is one of the most prestigious film schools in the nation, but Spike Lee soon felt that it was as conservative in its own way as Morehouse had been. As one of only a handful of blacks at the school, Spike felt pressure to conform, especially after he made his first student film in 1980. Called *The Answer*, it was a response to the 1915 silent-film classic *Birth of a Nation* by D. W. Griffith.

Griffith was considered a great filmmaker for his time, but whereas his film techniques were forward-looking, his politics were not. *Birth of a Nation* was set in the Reconstruction period that followed the Civil War, a time when federal troops occupied the former Confederate states, former Confederates were denied the vote, and free blacks and newly freed slaves were allowed to vote and hold political office. Blacks were shown as stereotypes: unable to think for themselves, frightened half to death by men in hooded robes (the early Ku Klux Klan). Spike Lee's student film was about a young black film student assigned to do a remake of the Griffith classic. It was very critical of *Birth of a Nation*, and Lee's professors were very critical of it.

They did not charge him with disrespect for Griffith. Rather, they criticized the film for being overambitious: First-year student films are only ten minutes long, and it *is* hard to remake *Birth of a Nation* in ten minutes. They also criticized Spike for not having yet mastered "film grammar," or the techniques of filmmaking. But Spike was convinced then, and still is, that the problem was more than his lack of technique; he believes they thought he was an upstart to criticize Griffith, the "father of cinema."

Students who complete the first year of the NYU film program must be selected to advance to the second year. Not everyone makes it, and for whatever reason, Spike almost did not make the cut.

Fortunately for both NYU and Spike Lee, he was invited to continue in the program, and he got along much better in his second year. He was awarded a teaching assistantship; in exchange for working in the school's equipment room, he got full tuition. His grandmother had given him tuition money for that year, so he used those funds to produce his films.

That same year Spike Lee began to work with Ernest Dickerson, another black student at the NYU film institute. Dickerson was several years older and had been an architecture student at all-black Howard University and then worked for five years as a medical illustrator before enrolling at NYU. His main interest was cinematography, the actual filming of motion pictures. In 1981 Dickerson photographed Spike's second-year student film, *Sarah*, the story of a Harlem family on Thanksgiving day.

Dickerson once described the attitude he, Spike Lee, and the few other blacks at NYU film school had toward filmmaking as a "fever." He would tell an interviewer, "We all had it *bad*. We were on a mission. We wanted to make films that captured the black experience in this country. Films about what we knew. We just couldn't wait."[6]

They were not alone. There were many budding black filmmakers in the country, like Robert Townsend, Euzhan Palcy, Charles Lane, and Warrington Hudlin. In 1979 Hudlin founded the Black Filmmaker Foundation. He and his friends would drive up to Harlem in a truck, hang a sheet on a tenement wall, and show black films in the streets. They wanted their work to be seen. Spike Lee also wanted his work to be seen; he showed *The Answer* at Leviticus, a black dance club in midtown Manhattan.

Lee formed a production company to make *Sarah*. He called his company Forty Acres and a Mule Filmworks. The reference is to the belief among freed slaves after the Civil War that the victorious Union government would grant that much land and a mule for plowing it to each emancipated slave. The grants were never made, and from time to time in the century-plus since the Civil War, various militant black leaders have demanded such "reparations," or repayment for all the work the slaves did without pay. Spike Lee's choice of the name indicated that he felt the U.S. film industry owed black people the opportunity to control the images of themselves on screen. Forty Acres and a Mule Filmworks is the name of the production company Lee has used for all his films.

Lee also commissioned his father to write an original score for his film, which was recorded by Bill Lee's musician friends. Having an original score distinguished *Sarah* from most other student films, which just used records for background music. Bill Lee also wrote a theme called "Forty Acres and a Mule" that played over the words in the opening credits.

Lee and Dickerson enjoyed working together on *Sarah* and determined to collaborate again. In 1982 during their third and final year at NYU, they worked together on Spike's master's thesis film, *Joe's Bed-Stuy Barbershop: We Cut Heads*. The film, set in Brooklyn's most well-known black ghetto, Bedford-Stuyvesant, was about a barber whose shop serves as a front for the neighborhood numbers racket, an illegal gambling game. The film was realistic but quietly funny. Spike had written the script the previous summer while visiting his grandmother in Atlanta. He'd showed his friend Monty Ross the script and was surprised when Ross offered to travel to New York from Atlanta to play the lead role. Spike hadn't even considered asking his friend to leave his wife and drop whatever he was doing, but he was pleased to have him involved in the project. Lee once again asked his father to write an original jazz score.

A much more polished work than *Sarah, Joe's Bed-Stuy Barbershop: We Cut Heads* brought Spike not only his master's degree in film from NYU but also his first serious recognition as a filmmaker. It won a student Academy Award from the Academy of Motion Picture Arts and Sciences in Hollywood and was the first student production to be selected for the prestigious "New Directors/New Films" series at New York's Lincoln Center. It was also aired on public television's *Independent Focus* series. It went on to be shown at film festivals in San Francisco and Los Angeles, California; Atlanta, Georgia; and Locarno, Switzerland.

In March 1983 the magazine *Variety* reviewed the film favorably, calling it a "friendly portrait of black folkways" with "convincing street language and wit." The review contrasted it to the blaxploitation gangster films and noted that Lee had turned his back on the sex and violence that had marked those films.

Most student-made films are never seen except by professors and fellow students. Spike Lee's film was still being seen and reviewed a year after he received his master's degree fron NYU. He was on his way.

3

Independent Filmmaker

Spike Lee received his master's de- gree from New York University's Institute of Film and Television in 1982, and based on the success of *Joe's Bed-Stuy Barbershop* was signed by both the International Creative Management and William Morris agencies. They were looking for a young black director because there had been some recent evidence of a slow resurgence of films about the black experience. In production at Columbia Pictures was the film version of *A Soldier's Story* (released in 1984), which had been a hit off-Broadway play. Warner Bros. had agreed to back *Purple Rain*, a film about the singer Prince, and to underwrite the film version of Alice Walker's book *The Color Purple* (released in 1985) directed by Steven Spielberg. The thinking at Morris and ICM was that if these movies did well at the box office, new black filmmakers would be in great demand.

Although, in theory, these agencies work for their clients, they are in the business of making money, which they do by taking a percentage of their clients' earnings. Thus they work harder for clients for whom it is easy to get work than they do for unknowns.

When Spike Lee signed on with these agencies, there was still little work available for black directors, and the agents at ICM and Morris did not, in his opinion, try very hard to find any for him, not even an afterschool TV special. It was not long before he realized that if he wanted to make films, he was going to have to go out and do it alone.

To support himself, since no job offers were coming in from the agencies, he went to work at First Run Features, a movie distribution house, cleaning and shipping film. Earning a salary of $200 per week, he could now afford to move out of his father's house, which he had wanted to do ever since Susan Kaplan Lee had moved in. His studio apartment with a kitchen on Myrtle Avenue was just around the corner from the family home, but it could be a world away if he wanted it to be. There, in his own place, he filled notebook after notebook with film ideas. He may have had no offers to do films and very little money, but he had a great deal of ambition.

He spent as much time as he could networking in New York's artistic community, introducing himself to whomever he thought he might need to know later on. The actor Larry Fishburne, who was then with the off-Broadway Negro Ensemble Company, told Stuart Mieher of the *New York Times Magazine* that he remembered standing in Washington Square Park in Greenwich Village one day when someone tapped him on the shoulder and said, "You're Larry Fishburne, you're a great actor. I'm Spike Lee, and I make films."[1] Not long after that, Lee made his first foray into film production. He wrote a script for a film to be titled *The Messenger* about a bicycle messenger in New York City who is forced to become the head of his family after his mother dies of a heart attack. He then set about finding the money to produce it.

Independent Filmmaker

Spike Lee now says that the project was overambitious, but having just come out of film school he had no idea of the harsh realities of raising money to make films. His first dose of reality was learning that funding sources would not give him money outright. They would only give it to a not-for-profit tax-exempt organization. So Lee went to Warrington Hudlin, founder of the Black Filmmaker Foundation, which had distributed two of his student films, and got Hudlin to agree that his foundation would serve as the agent for the grants.

With a $20,000 grant from the American Film Institute, which was not payable until actual production began, a $10,000 grant from the Jerome Foundation, money borrowed from his grandmother, and the promise to raise the rest of the necessary financial backing from a friend of the family, who would be credited as the film's producer, Lee began the preproduction phase in the summer of 1984.

Preproduction on a film involves such things as finding locations, finalizing the script, and hiring a cast and crew. Ordinarily, a producer waits until most of the money is in hand even to begin preproduction. Spike Lee did not wait. He had already formed his own production company, Forty Acres and a Mule Filmworks. He was president, and Monty Ross, his friend in Atlanta, was vice president. He had also already designed a *Messenger* T-shirt for the cast and crew to wear and to sell when the film was released. He had learned from his internship in Hollywood that he wanted to control all aspects of his films.

He went scouting for locations. He hired a crew. He went ahead and cast actors for the roles. He did not have enough money to pay union actors, so he worked out a deal, or so he thought, with the Screen Actors Guild, the union that represents professional actors. He sought a waiver of their usual rules based on the argument that his film was not commercial. Such waivers are often granted for low-budget, independent films, and Lee believed his qualified.

But still the promised money did not come through, and Lee spent sleepless nights worrying about what he was going to do. His stomach churned so much that he could not eat. He lost weight. He could not pay his own bills. Then, when the film had been in preproduction for eight weeks, the Screen Actors Guild refused to allow the waiver, saying the film was too commercial. Spike Lee was convinced the real reason was racism.

He had already spent $40,000 paying a crew and nonunion actors, and suddenly he found himself with just four days in which to recast the film with union actors. He could not do it and had to give up the project.

"It was and still is the most painful experience of my professional life," he wrote in *Five for Five*. Having failed to make his film was the least of it. What really bothered him was that he had let down so many people. His grandmother Zimmie, who had put him through college and film school, had lost $20,000. "It was hard for me to face people," Lee wrote; "folks were mad as hell; and they had a right to be because they lost money and had turned down *real money, real employment* to work on a nonexistent film."[2] One day, soon after he had shut down production on the film, Lee sat in a bathtub filled with water and cried. The man who never cried—not even at his mother's funeral—now cried a full hour. He wondered why all this had happened to him when he didn't deserve it.

Crying was the best thing for him to do, for once he had cried himself out, he felt better. Soon he had regained his fighting spirit. The whole *Messenger* fiasco had been a good learning experience for him, he decided. He would never make the same mistakes again. The next time around he would write a script with just a few characters, use inexpensive neighborhood locations, and plan for a small budget. Most important, he would not even begin preproduction until he had the money in the bank. And, he promised himself, the following summer he would be ready to make that doable film.

Lee was soon hard at work writing the script for his next film. This time, he was determined to come up with a script that could be done for as little money as possible but that would make as much money as possible. It had been three years since he had made a film, and he was anxious to get back into the business of his dreams.

While he wanted his film to make money, Lee also wanted it to make a statement, to say something he felt should be said. He believed that black love was noticeably absent from the silver screen, and his film was going to be about love, with lots of shots of black couples kissing. In fact, black love and love scenes between blacks were just about all the film that he eventually called *She's Gotta Have It* was about. The major character is a young, attractive, independent black woman named Nola Darling. Her birthday is the same as that of Malcolm X, the charismatic black leader who was assassinated in 1965, and she uses her talent as a graphic designer to protest the senseless killing of two black New Yorkers by police. But the main plot is about the way she manages to juggle three boyfriends with wildly different personalities.

Lee intended to cut as many corners as possible to keep his budget down. *She's Gotta Have It* would have very few characters, local Brooklyn settings, and no sets or costumes. It would be shot in black and white, because Lee could not afford color. He used 16-mm rather than 35-mm film, because 16 mm is less expensive.

But even an inexpensive film costs money, and Spike Lee had very little. He managed to secure an $18,000 grant from the New York State Council on the Arts and a $500 grant from the Brooklyn Arts and Cultural Association. He expected to get the $10,000 grant from the Jerome Foundation transferred from the ill-fated *Messenger* project to *She's Gotta Have It*. He had hoped to do the same with the $20,000 grant he had received from the American Film Institute for *The Messenger*, but he was not allowed to do so.

His grandmother again came through with money. Friends contributed small amounts, sometimes as little as $100. For a time, Lee decided the best way to raise the needed money was to form a limited partnership and sell shares in his film for $15,000 apiece. But he wasn't successful in attracting many investors, and eventually he decided he did not want to give up control of his film anyway. He was determined to remain as independent as possible. Still, when the spring of 1985 arrived and he was ready to start preproduction, he did not have all the money he needed in the bank.

Lee advertised in the entertainment trade newspaper *Back Stage* for actors and actresses to audition for the few roles in the film. A pretty young woman with short hair and a button nose named Tracy Camila Johns, whose previous acting experience was stage roles with the Negro Ensemble Company, got the part of the lead character, Nola Darling, after sending in a head shot (photograph of her face) and then reading for the part. Tommy Redmond Hicks played Jamie Overstreet, the salt-of-the-earth type who wanted to marry Nola. John Canada Terrell played Greer Childs, a suave model who wanted an equally attractive woman to show off. This time Spike managed to persuade the actors' union to grant him deferrals so he didn't have to pay the wages actors normally commanded. Primarily as a way to save money, Lee cast himself as the third boyfriend, Mars Blackmon, a rapping streetwise character. Lee's grandmother Zimmie had suggested the name Mars for the character because she'd had an uncle named Mars who she said was crazy.

Bill Lee wrote the score, as he had for Spike's student films and for the ill-fated *Messenger*. Bill Lee and Susan Kaplan had gotten married and had a son, Arnold Tone Kaplan Lee. But that had not softened Spike's attitude toward his father. He and his father could barely speak to one another without arguing. Still, Spike Lee believed in family, and he was determined that his father would write the music for his film. Brother David, who had majored in photography at Yale University, filmed the opening credit sequence and winter montage (patchwork of pictures). Spike hired his youngest brother, Cinque, as a production assistant. As if there were not enough work for the Lee family, Joie Lee (she'd changed the spelling of her name from Joy in junior high school) was offered a bit part as a former roommate of the lead character.

Joie had attended Sarah Lawrence College for two semesters but had found in its primarily white student body a mere "extension of St. Ann's." She believes that if her mother had been alive, she would probably have attended a black college. She dropped out and spent a couple of years working for nonprofit arts foundations and trying to figure out what to do with her life. In the spring of 1985 she was working at a company called Film/Video Arts. She had never seriously considered acting, although while at St. Ann's she and her brother David had appeared in a student version of the musical *H.M.S. Pinafore* and she had sung a soprano part. Then in 1985 her brother Spike sent her the script for *She's Gotta Have It* and suggested she read for the part of Clorinda Bradford, Nola Darling's former roommate. She got the part and, working with an actress friend from the St. Ann's days, managed to perform to her brother's and her own satisfaction a role that consisted mainly of staring into the camera and delivering a monologue about lesbianism.

In spite of the fact that he had his sister, his father, and two brothers working on his film, Lee did not feel emotionally close to his family. When not working together, they rarely saw each other. Spike insisted he did not choose them to work with him out of a sense of closeness but because they were the best people for the job. But he may not have been able to admit to himself that working with his family, although they were talented, was a way to do what he knew his mother would have wanted, and that was to keep the family close. It was certainly what his grandmother wanted; she frequently scolded him for not knowing more about his brothers' and sister's lives.

Lisa Jones served as another production assistant. Daughter of the poet and playwright LeRoi Jones, who had subsequently changed his name to Amiri Baraka, Lisa also worked with Spike on a journal of the making of *She's Gotta Have It*, which would be published along with the film.

Ernest Dickerson did the cinematography. Since graduating from NYU, he had worked on John Sayles's *The Brother from Another Planet* and Michael Schultz's *Krush Groove*. He could now command a high salary, but he took a salary deferment to work with

Spike. Monty Ross came up from Atlanta to serve as production supervisor, also taking a salary deferment.

Although there were just four main characters and a couple of minor ones, there were bit parts. To save money, Lee cast his girlfriend, Cheryl Burr, his father, Monty Ross, and even Ernest Dickerson in these parts.

At the end of June 1985, Lee asked for a month off from his job at First Run Features. His boss told him he wasn't sure if the firm would need him after that time. In effect, he was fired. Now he had to worry about how to pay his rent and his utility bills in addition to worrying about how to pay for his film.

Spike had long since graduated from NYU, but he secured permission to use the school's facilities. He conducted his first script read-throughs at the school. Once he felt sure that the actors knew their lines and understood the motivations of their characters, they all went "on location."

He thought he was going to cut more corners by using a friend's van. But the Teamsters Union, which controlled all vehicles on New York film shoots, made him pay a fine for doing so, which defeated the purpose. There were all sorts of other problems, many of them money problems. He did not realize he had to buy insurance on the camera equipment he was renting, but managed to get it for 10 percent down. Other problems were due to the inexperience of the director and production supervisor, like forgetting to arrange for electrical power on location. Shooting officially began on July 5, 1985, and was completed in twelve days. The primary location was a large loft above the Ferry Bank restaurant in the Fort Greene section of Brooklyn. The windows didn't open, and the temperature in the loft sometimes reached 100 degrees without the lights on.

Once the hot camera lights were turned on, it was unbearably hot. Everyone was glad when they moved outside for the scenes in Fort Greene Park nearby. The one extravagance Lee agreed to, to set the scene for his film, was a specially made "loving bed" for the character Nola. His production designer, Wynn Thomas, talked him into paying $100 to have a bed made that featured a sort of latticework headboard covered with candles.

It was the second most nerve-wracking time of Spike Lee's life. In addition to all the problems of working with inexperienced actors and production people, there were constant money worries. Every day, after shooting was done, he and Monty Ross looked at each other and wondered where they were going to get the money for the next day's shooting. They called or wrote to everyone they knew, asking them to send money—any amount of money. Every day, someone would be dispatched from the set to go back to Lee's apartment to see if any checks had come in and then rush them to the bank, hoping they would clear in time.

Shooting the film was just one part of the filmmaking process. Ahead of Lee were months of work editing the film, for he did not have the money to hire a professional film editor. He rented a six-reel film-editing machine and spent hours in his apartment cutting and splicing. Each time he had a rough cut he had to get it processed, and that cost money. At one point, the film-processing laboratory Lee was using threatened to auction off the negative for the film unless he could come up with the $2,000 he owed by five o'clock that afternoon. Fortunately, Nelson George, a music critic who had become interested in the project, agreed to pay the entire bill for him.

Spike Lee continued to borrow money from anyone who would

give it, including his girlfriend, Cheryl Burr. His grandmother was constantly sending him money, for there were times when he was a month behind on his rent or facing the cutoff of his electricity.

When there was no money for final editing that winter, Lee showed a rough cut to anyone who would watch it, hoping thereby to raise the money necessary to complete the film. NYU, his alma mater, agreed that he could use its small movie theater to show the rough cut to an audience of artists and executives in the entertainment industry. Lee gave up his usual attire of jeans and a sweatshirt and dressed in a suit for the occasion. When the film was over, he stepped to the front of the theater and said, "I'm Spike Lee and I hope that you liked the film, and I'll be calling you soon about becoming financially involved and helping us complete it."[3] By means of such tactics, Lee managed to raise the money needed for the final phases of production, including enough to get the 16-mm film blown up to 35 mm. By the time *She's Gotta Have It* had been edited and was ready for distribution, it had cost a total of $175,000, which was peanuts by Hollywood standards.

There was one more hurdle. To expose his film to the widest possible audience, Lee had to get an *R*-rating from the Film Board. As a condition of granting that rating, the Film Board insisted he shorten one of his sex scenes. Lee did so but grumbled about it, saying that the sex scenes between a white man and woman in the film *9^1/$_2$ Weeks*, which had recently received an *R*-rating, were much more deserving of an *X*-rating than what he had to cut. In his mind, it was another example of racism.

When *She's Gotta Have It* was ready, Spike Lee was also ready with a T-shirt and the manuscript for *Spike Lee's She's Gotta Have It: Inside Guerrilla Filmmaking*, his book about the making of the film that would be illustrated with photographs by his brother David. Keeping a journal while making the film was a smart marketing idea. It was also natural for Spike Lee, who had inherited a keen sense of history from his parents, to record his trials and tribulations and, ultimately, his triumph.

Now he wanted to make sure the film was seen by as many film distributors as possible. He submitted *She's Gotta Have It* to the San Francisco Film Festival, where it was screened in March of 1986. The film received a standing ovation and requests for distribution rights from a number of film companies. Island Films eventually won out. Lee chose Island because of the company's innovative ideas for marketing the film, including selling *She's Gotta Have It* T-shirts, posters, and buttons at theaters and releasing a soundtrack album. Also, Island agreed to let Lee keep music publishing rights and sequel rights, and to have the right of consultation with respect to all marketing and advertising.

Next, Lee took *She's Gotta Have It* to the Cannes Film Festival on the French Riviera. Every year for two weeks Cannes becomes the capital of the international film industry, a magnet for producers, directors, and stars. That year, *She's Gotta Have It* was awarded the Prix de la Jeunesse (Young Director's Prize). It was a heady time for Spike Lee, who now believed all the anxiety over money to produce the film was worth it.

August 8, 1986, was the film's official opening in the United States at New York's Cinema Studio, and the reviews were mostly favorable. The film had a lot of sex, as Lee had intended, but it also had a lot of humor. It poked fun at the things many men will tell women in order to get them into bed and turned the usual male hunter/female prey arrangement on its end. It showed, according to novelist Terry McMillan writing in an essay in *Five for Five,* "how wimpy men can be when it comes to a woman."[4] The reviewer for the *New York Times* said it was "technically messy" but that it had "a touch of the classic." The reviewer for the *Village Voice* said it was "an almost unprecedented work—an all-black comedy of manners." Wrote the reviewer for *People,* "So much cinematic invention has been lavished on this film it sometimes spins out of control, but Lee's joy in making movies informs every frame. No director in 1986 made a more exciting feature debut."[5] Other reviewers singled out Spike Lee's acting, and several accused him of stealing his own show. Joie Lee's brief appearance received good reviews, as did Ernest Dickerson's cinematography and Bill Lee's score.

But more important than reviews in the career of a young filmmaker are box-office receipts. *She's Gotta Have It* earned $1.8 million in its first three weeks. Spike Lee felt vindicated. As he told an interviewer for the *New York Times* that November, "The whole point is that you can take an unknown, all-black cast and put them in a story that comes from a black experience, and all kinds of people will come to see it if it's a good film. I wish Hollywood would get that message."

But in truth Lee was relieved that the film had done as well as it had. He did not think much of the acting, and admitted to himself that the actors had been miscast and that he had much to learn about how to work with actors. Additionally, every time he remembered the anxiety he had felt every day about where the next nickel to make the film was going to come from, he felt a little sick. Although the film eventually brought in nearly $8 million at the box office, even today he cannot bring himself to watch it.

One other good thing that came from that film was his contract to do commercials for Nike footwear. Two men from the advertising firm that made commercials for Nike saw *She's Gotta Have It*. They noticed that Mars Blackmon, the character Lee played, wore Nike Air Jordans and considered Michael Jordan of the Chicago Bulls his hero. They got in touch with Lee and asked him to do a commercial with Michael Jordan. Lee jumped at the opportunity, not only for the money and for the exposure it would give his film, but also because he was a great fan of basketball and of Michael Jordan.

In addition to appearing in a Nike commercial, Lee filmed a music video for a new album by the musician Miles Davis and a short piece for the television program *Saturday Night Live.* But these projects were just something to do until he started work on his next major motion picture.

Meanwhile, he was trying to adjust to his "overnight" fame. Having splurged on an answering machine, he wondered if he shouldn't have gotten one with room for more messages. Every time he got home, the machine was filled. He heard from friends he didn't even know he had. His mail was voluminous as well, including a heavily perfumed note from one woman who said they had played doctor at school and wasn't it time for him to have a physical.

Lee was amazed by what fame and money did for his image. He was not used to being seen as a heartthrob, to having women practically throw themselves at him. In fact, in all his life he'd had just one serious, long-term relationship. He and Cheryl Burr had gone together for about a year before breaking up in 1985. She had been the one to end the relationship, but Spike couldn't blame her. He'd borrowed money from her to make *She's Gotta Have It* and was unable to pay it back when she needed it. But more than money had been at issue. For months and months he had been so obsessed with his film that he hadn't had time to pay attention to her. Movies were his first love, and he did not regret having made his film at the expense of his romantic relationship. He told himself there would be time enough for love and marriage and a family after he had made his mark in the film world.

4

Musical Maker

***She's Gotta Have It* was barely in re-**
lease when Spike Lee began planning his next film. Based on the
success of *She's Gotta Have It,* Island Films, the distributor, offered
Lee $4 million for his next picture. That was big money for a young
filmmaker. Lee was about to undertake a far more ambitious film—a
musical this time. He was going to do his own big musical like those
he had loved as a child.

Musicals, whether Broadway shows or Hollywood films, cost a
great deal of money. The maker of a musical has to pay someone to
do the score and someone else to do the choreography; one also has
to hire singers and dancers. But Spike Lee wanted to do a musical.
The screenplay he had written shortly after graduating from NYU,
about student life at an all-black college in the South, could best be
told through song and dance.

To prepare for actual shooting, Lee and Ernest Dickerson
spent hours in the fall of 1986 watching old Metro-Goldwyn-Mayer
musicals as well as *West Side Story* (1961), Lee's favorite musical
of all time. They studied the bright colors, the intense lighting, the

way the dancers were photographed. They planned actual shots by drawing storyboards, diagrams of how certain shots should look through the camera. Part of the reason for such thoroughness was that when actual shooting began there would be a plan, and they could keep the time for actual shooting to a minimum.

Meanwhile, Lee was working on the story for the film, editing the screenplay, "Homecoming," that he had written several years before. Although Mission College, the college in the screenplay, was fictional, it was based on Morehouse College and Lee's perceptions of its culture while he was a student there.

One of the observations that had most troubled him was the students' concern with differences in complexion. It seemed to him that the last thing black Americans needed to do to themselves was divide themselves by skin color. But at Morehouse, as in much of the rest of African-American society, the lighter-skinned blacks felt superior to the darker-complected ones. It was racism within the race.

In his script for the film, set on the campus of the fictitious Mission College, Lee focused on two groups of students he called "jigaboos" and "wannabees." The jigaboos were the dark-skinned blacks. The term is derisive, like "jungle bunny," and is often used by racist whites. But, like "nigger," it is also used among blacks, and Spike Lee was not afraid to say so. In the film, the women jigaboos were called the Naturals; they wore their hair in the Afro style also called a natural. The men were Da Fellas, the campus radicals, who were conducting a campaign to get the trustees of the school to divest themselves of their investments in South Africa, which at the time was still operating under the system of racial classification called apartheid. The opening scene of the film was an antiapartheid demonstration. Da Fellas also claimed to be against separation of the Mission students by color and class, but they were dark skinned and at times seemed to dislike other students just because they were light complected.

The second group of students, the wannabees, were the lighter-complected students who wanted to "be white." The male wannabees were the members of Gamma Phi Gamma, the most powerful fraternity on campus, and the women, the Gamma Rays, were members of the sister organization associated with Gamma Phi Gamma.

As part of his marketing strategy, Lee decided to get as many well-known actors as he could to appear in the film. As the leader of the campus radicals, Lee cast Larry Fishburne, whom he had approached some years earlier in Washington Square Park. Fishburne had starred in both the Negro Ensemble Company's off-Broadway production of *A Soldier's Play* and in the movie version, called *A Soldier's Story*, that had been released in 1984. A fine actor, he expected a high salary, and Lee finally had the money to pay an actor of Fishburne's caliber.

For the part of Coach Odum, Lee cast the veteran actor Ossie Davis, who with his actress wife, Ruby Dee, had taken a special interest in Lee as a young filmmaker with great promise. Originally, Vanessa Williams, the former Miss America who had been forced to give up her crown after pornographic photographs she had posed for years before were revealed, was to have played the role of Jane Toussaint, one of the light-complected Gamma Rays. But once she read the script, she pulled out. The official reason given was "artistic differences," and she was replaced. The same thing happened with Phyllis Stickney, who was to have played one of the jigaboos.

Jasmine Guy, of the television show *A Different World,* played a Gamma Ray.

Veteran actors Joe Seneca, Ellen Holly, and Art Evans played school administrators and faculty. Musician Branford Marsalis, for whom Lee had directed a music video, was cast as one of Da Fellas.

Once again, Lee cast himself in one of the roles. He did not particularly enjoy acting; this was more of a marketing move. He realized that people would go to see his movie just to see him, the Mars Blackmon character from the Nike commercials. He cast himself as Half-Pint, who was a jigaboo in skin color and background but wanted to be a wannabee and so was pledging the Gamma Phi Gamma fraternity.

Lee cast his sister, Joie, as Lizzie Life, one of the jigaboos. Joie had not continued her acting career after appearing in *She's Gotta Have It.* Instead, she had spent a year in Seattle, Washington, just hanging out. Back in New York, she had auditioned for a role in a segment of the television series *The Cosby Show* but had been told her acting was "too heavy." Around that time, her brother Spike suggested that she enroll at NYU film school and study with Alice Spivak, who had taught him. He would pay her tuition. Joie followed his advice and decided to pursue an acting career.

Lee cast his younger brother, twenty-one-year-old Cinque, in the small role of Buckwheat. Cinque worked on the crew as well.

Other members of the Lee family also worked on the film. David did the still photography, Bill Lee wrote the score, and Spike's aunt, Consuela Lee Morehead, a pianist, served as assistant musical director.

With more money than he'd ever had to work with before, Lee had a great time doing preproduction work on the film, which he had decided to call *School Daze*. In fact, he was spending so much money that Island Films executives feared that the film would go over budget. In January 1987, before work on the film went any further, they pulled out.

Now Lee had to find another backer for his film. The very next day he began calling other studios, and within two days he had worked out a $6-million deal with Columbia Pictures. He flew to Los Angeles for meetings and the signing of papers and was treated by Columbia Pictures to great seats at the Super Bowl.

Spike Lee was somebody important now. Stevie Wonder had written a song for his film. The Reverend Jesse Jackson delivered a prayer on the set in Atlanta, asking for the project's success. The administrations at Morehouse and Spelman Colleges had been pleased to offer their facilities to him.

But there would be plenty of problems for Spike Lee in the making of *School Daze*. After three weeks of shooting, word apparently reached the Morehouse authorities that the film was not going to portray the school in a favorable light. Reports reached the office of Morehouse president Hugh Morris Gloster that the script included obscene words as well as an emphasis on color consciousness at the school. Gloster was concerned that parents would judge the school on the basis of what they saw in the film. Lee was given an ultimatum: Unless he let Morehouse authorities read the script, he would not be allowed to continue shooting at the campus. Lee refused and pulled out his entire company. Filming of *School Daze* was completed at the graduate school of nearby Atlanta University.

The United Negro College Fund, of which Morehouse was a member, was to have sponsored a benefit premiere of the film. But once word of its controversial subject matter got out, plans for the benefit were canceled. Lee was not surprised. He did feel, however, that the UNCF was cutting off its nose to spite its face, since it needed the money the benefit would have brought in.

Lee had trouble finding students to work as unpaid extras. Another film was being shot in Atlanta, and he found himself competing with that other production for student extras.

In spite of these problems, work on the film proceeded. The plot was thin, and the story line served primarily to make the major point Lee wanted to get across: Color prejudice is divisive and destructive. Sometimes the actors wondered if that was the reason Lee seemed to give them so little direction. He was not a "hands-on" director who coached his actors' every move. Instead, he seemed often not to be paying any attention to what they were doing. He'd have his back turned and his eyes closed as a scene was being shot. Stuart Mieher of the *New York Times Magazine* visited the set while shooting was in progress and noted that Lee's most conspicuous direction of the day was to tell Larry Fishburne, "Larry, the way you did it the first time was really better."[1]

Fishburne told Mieher, "Spike really doesn't communicate verbally with the actors a lot. I'll look at him like I'm wondering, 'Hey, am I doing O.K.?' and he nods." He added, "I don't think he's developed all the skills he might need to communicate with actors."[2]

Lee took Fishburne's comments to heart and determined to communicate better with the actors in his next film. Still, he planned to give them a great deal of room to improvise. His style of directing was to trust the actors to do what they were being paid for and to let them experiment with their roles. If someone wanted to try a line another way, or even change lines, he didn't mind, as long as the changes were in keeping with his vision of the film. Lee did more directing when the cameras were off. He urged the actors whose characters belonged to different factions to become friends with their on-screen friends and avoid their on-screen enemies. In that way, the different groups developed a cohesiveness that was reflected in their acting.

In *School Daze* the characters and the story line were not as important as the points Lee wanted to make through his opening scenes and his musical numbers. The opening scenes were of the Middle Passage, the journey African slaves made aboard slave ships from Africa to the New World. It was a short lesson in black history using old prints and drawings, with a sound track of spirituals, that was meant to show how blacks came to be so separated from each other. There were other serious parts of the film. But Lee chose to make most of his points through humor. There was a big musical number at Madame Re Re's beauty salon called "Straight and Nappy" in which the jigaboos and the wannabees danced and sang in competition with one another. Another number, "Da Butt," took place at a wild fraternity party. And the finale, "Wake Up," was a clear message to blacks, young college blacks in particular, to stop going around in a "daze" and wake up to the idea that they had better get together.

When final editing was done, Lee was pleased with the way the film turned out. But he was prepared for criticism. He knew he had touched on some sensitive issues. Also, he realized that he, and *School Daze,* would be judged by a different standard than he and *She's Gotta Have It* had been. He was no longer an exciting new filmmaker but one who would be expected to prove that he could make more than one successful, and profitable, film. He wasn't worried. He was certain that *School Daze* would make money.

Well before the film was in final edit, Lee began to market a T-shirt that quoted words of Dr. Martin Luther King, Jr., referring to when black people would enjoy equality in the United States: "How long, not long." On Lee's T-shirts the slogan was "How Long, Not Long, Not Long, February '88." The date referred to the scheduled release date for the film. But in early January 1988 Lee's whole marketing vision was dealt a setback. Executives at Columbia Pictures informed him that they wanted to delay the release of the film.

The ostensible reason was that Lorimar Pictures had scheduled the release of *Action Jackson*, starring Carl Weathers and Vanity, on the same day as *School Daze* was to be released. Columbia did not think that *School Daze*, which was being billed as a musical comedy, could compete with this action-adventure. Spike Lee was furious. In his opinion, *Action Jackson* was just an updated 1970s blaxploitation film and no competition for *School Daze*. "What that says to me," he wrote in his journal on January 5, 1988, "is that Columbia sees Black people as one monolithic audience. . . . We all go to the same movies and we all have the same taste."[3]

By that time, Lee was losing patience with Columbia Pictures. The head of the studio when he'd signed on, David Puttnam, was out, and the new head, Dawn Steel, had no special interest in a picture that she'd had nothing to do with. "Steely Dawn," as Lee called her, and Lee did not get along from the beginning. The trouble was, she now had control over the marketing plan and budget for *School Daze*, and the more they argued the smaller that plan and budget became. Lee had envisioned ads in black magazines like

Ebony and *Essence.* Columbia said no. Instead, the company wanted Lee to go on an extended tour to promote the film. Lee did not like traveling and especially did not like the idea of an extended tour. In the end, however, he agreed to a two-week tour, realizing that if he did not promote his film it would not get promoted. Besides, he told himself, while on the tour he could get a lot of work done on the script for his next film, ideas for which he'd already started jotting down.

Lee did win one point with Columbia. *School Daze* was released on February 12, just four days later than originally planned, along with merchandise like caps and T-shirts, and a book published by Simon and Schuster entitled *Uplift the Race: The Construction of School Daze.*

The film received mixed critical reviews. Critics applauded Lee's attempts to reveal the black college experience. They also praised his performance as Half-Pint, the eager fraternity pledge. But they thought that the themes in the film were not well developed. And they criticized many of the musical numbers as being overambitious and technically weak. The general consensus was that Spike Lee didn't have enough experience to do a musical.

Some criticized his portrayal of women, saying he had failed to develop any of the women characters, who were just symbols. Lee was charged with treating women as objects, and primarily sexual objects. In response, Lee pointed to all the women who had worked behind the scenes on the film, including the executive producer, the coproducer-attorney, the production coordinator, the second assistant director, the costume designer, the casting director, and the unit publicist. He believed that his hiring practices were proof that he saw women as real people.

Lee was very thin-skinned, and some of the criticism began to affect him. When film critic Janet Maslin, in an article in the *New York Times*, questioned his technical abilities as a filmmaker, he shot off a bitter letter to the newspaper calling her comments racist and demanding that Maslin never review his films again. He ended with the line, "I bet she can't even dance, does she have rhythm?"[4]

Lee also went on the defensive about the music in his film, especially about the number "Da Butt." Many people complained that the title, which refers to the human bottom, and the dance were in poor taste. Both Lee and Marcus Miller, whom Lee had commissioned to write the song "Da Butt," wrote open letters to *R & B Report*, a music industry magazine published in Hollywood, which were published in the March 14, 1988, issue. Miller's was primarily in defense of his song; Lee's was in defense of both the song and the film:

> Dear *School Daze* and "Da Butt" critics:
>
> As far as I'm concerned you can make your own movies and your own records if you don't like mine, you ignorant, handkerchief-wearing, chicken-and-biscuit-eating Negroes. You same Negroes who are offended by this movie and by "Da Butt" probably also think James Brown [the singer] is not a positive image. Then please watch *A Different World*. That probably fits your idea of positive, ideal black people at a positive, ideal college. But *A Different World* is not the kind of black college I attended. (It's fake.) I made the film I wanted to make. The film turned out the way I envisioned it. And it's tuff if it offends some of you.
>
> All that stuff in the movie has happened. The only

thing that was slightly exaggerated was the skin-color controversy between light-skinned blacks and dark-skinned blacks.

Just because I present problems, some people expect me to solve them. That's really unrealistic. It's a burden I won't assume. I am thirty years old. I don't have all the answers, and don't pretend to. That's not my job. We intended this film to provoke discussion, which is what it's doing. That was our task. And we performed it. If we don't address problems, they don't get talked about and solved.

As for "Da Butt." Some of you say that song shouldn't have been what it is. People kill me: the people who criticize "Da Butt" probably can't even dance.

When fifty black films come out every year, maybe you'll stop expecting me to be all things to everybody. I am one filmmaker. I will continue to make quality films. That is all I promise. WAKE UP!

Sincerely,
Spike Lee

In spite of the less than rave reviews, and in spite of Lee's feeling that Columbia Pictures did not properly promote the film, *School Daze* was a box-office success and made *Variety*'s list of the top-ten moneymaking films in March 1988. Thousands of young blacks went to see it, and even adopted the dance that was in the movie's final dance scene. Naturally, this new dance craze was called "Da Butt."

In an ironic twist, seeing *School Daze* didn't turn young blacks off black colleges at all. On the contrary, it made them want to go to a black college, for the film portrayed a social life that they envied. Once black college administrators had seen the film, they realized it was an excellent one to show at benefit fund-raisers. So did many black organizations.

Clearly, blacks, not to mention whites, were going to movie theaters to see Spike Lee movies, and Spike Lee was one of the most talked-about young directors in the film world. Some critics compared him to Woody Allen, primarily because of his offbeat sense of humor. Lee did not like that comparison at all. His role models were Akira Kurosawa, Martin Scorsese, and Gordon Parks. The only similarity he could see between Allen and himself was that they were both New Yorkers. He criticized Allen for making pictures set in New York—which has many minorities—but with no minority characters. And he did not believe that Allen addressed controversial issues, as he himself had the courage to do. Allen's films were very personal, rather like self-analysis. It could be said that until this time, so were Spike Lee's. But he was already thinking about a film that would take a larger view and address the most controversial issue of our times, racism between blacks and whites.

5

Spike Lee Does the Right Thing

Spike Lee began making notes for *Do the Right Thing* on the morning of Christmas Day, 1987. Although it was the proverbial "cold day in December," he was thinking heat—hot, sweltering heat. He was thinking of the hottest day of the summer, when people who could not afford air-conditioning woke up drenched in sweat and got shorter tempers as the day grew longer. He was thinking about the optimum conditions for a race riot (the worst race riots in New York, and in history, have occurred in the hottest months), and he was thinking about a racial incident in Howard Beach, in Queens, New York, just a year earlier. One evening a group of three blacks were driving through the neighborhood when they had trouble with their car. They saw a pizza parlor nearby and went there to use the telephone. They were confronted by a crowd of whites wielding baseball bats and shouting epithets at the "niggers" who had dared come into their neighborhood. The three blacks took off running. Two were savagely beaten. The third, Michael Griffith, ran onto the highway and was struck and killed by an oncoming car driven by the son of a policeman.

The bald racism of the incident infuriated blacks, as did the outcome of the trials of the whites. In spite of eyewitness testimony by one of the black men, Cedric Sandiford, the members of the white mob who were convicted were found guilty of manslaughter, not murder, of misdemeanors, not felonies. A local black leader, the Reverend Al Sharpton, led black marchers through Howard Beach to protest the racism of the predominantly Italian neighborhood. In scattered incidents around the city, blacks attacked whites, shouting "Howard Beach," as if to say they were personally avenging the attack on the three black men. In Spike Lee's opinion, if the weather had not been so cold—if the Howard Beach incident had occurred in the heat of summer—full-scale rioting might have resulted.

Lee got to thinking about the tension between blacks and Italians, whose working-class youth seemed to be especially racist. From the Howard Beach incident, and Lee's thinking about it, came the script for *Do the Right Thing*. It would be his most political film yet and would address the issue of racism head-on. And because it did so, it would be his first film to include major white characters as well as black ones.

Even before *School Daze* had been released, Lee knew which black actors he wanted for the film: Ossie Davis, and perhaps his wife, Ruby Dee; Larry Fishburne, Giancarlo Esposito, and Bill Nunn, all of whom had been in *School Daze*. Lee knew he would cast himself in a significant role. In all the prerelease showings of *School Daze*, his character, Half-Pint, had scored high with audiences. If audiences wanted to see more of him, he intended to oblige.

There would be a part for his sister, Joie, and perhaps a part for his youngest brother, Cinque. (As it turned out, Cinque, who had attended Yale Drama School and wanted a career as an actor, was offered a role in the film *Mystery Train* directed by Jim Jarmusch, who had been at NYU with Spike, and was too involved in that project to appear in his brother's film.)

Although he had no trouble visualizing actors for the black people's roles, the roles played by whites were another matter. He had not worked with white actors before, and he wasn't worried about doing so. But he did feel that he would cast those roles only in New York. His reason was that he wanted to cast white actors who felt comfortable around black people, and he believed he could most easily find those white actors in New York.

By the first of March, Lee had completed the first draft of his screenplay and was ready to show it to various studio heads whom he wanted to interest in backing *Do the Right Thing*. He planned to ask for a budget of $10 million. One studio he did not even approach was Columbia. He was furious that the studio had reneged, as he saw it, on its promises to market *School Daze*. He wanted to interest Touchstone Pictures in his project, but he realized that that studio was upset with him for going with Columbia when it had made a serious bid for *School Daze*.

Paramount Pictures expressed some interest in the project, but its executives were worried that the last scene, in which the black people in the neighborhood burn down the pizza parlor, might incite black moviegoers to riot. A recently released film, black director John Singleton's *Boyz N the Hood*, had been charged with inciting violence by gang members in some cities such as Los Angeles. Spike Lee thought those fears were ridiculous and refused to change the end of the script.

Lee was beginning to worry that he would never get *Do the*

Right Thing off the ground. It was very important to him to follow *School Daze* with another film right away, for in recent times no black filmmaker had been able to do one film after another the way white directors did. While he waited for Paramount to make up its mind, he approached other Hollywood studios, including Universal and Orion. He also shot a music video for Steel Pulse and one for "I Can Only Be Me," a song from *School Daze*.

Meanwhile, Lee cast the white roles in the film. In the middle of May, he and the actor Danny Aiello went to a Yankees baseball game together and, between plays, talked about their childhoods. Aiello had grown up in the South Bronx and was comfortable around blacks. Not long afterward, it became official that Aiello would play Sal, the owner of the pizza parlor. Richard Edson and John Turturro, who had grown up in a black neighborhood in Queens, were lined up to play Sal's sons, Pino and Vito.

Lee was now busily at work on the second draft of the script, fleshing out many of the characters and plot lines. Ossie Davis and Ruby Dee provided ideas for the backgrounds of their characters, Da Mayor and Mother Sister, and Lee incorporated many of their suggestions into the script.

By May 23, Universal Studios had refused to go for a budget any higher than $6.5 million, when Lee insisted he had to have at least $7.5 million. But he was down to the wire with nowhere else to go. He signed with Universal.

Given that comparatively small budget, Lee had to adjust his shooting schedule from nine weeks to eight. He would have preferred to use a nonunion crew, but doing so risked incurring the wrath of the unions. If he wanted to shoot his film in New York, he realized he had to keep the unions happy. Trouble was, the unions had very few black members, and it was important to Spike Lee to have as many blacks behind the scenes as there were in front of the camera. He had publicly criticized black stars like Eddie Murphy for not using their power to get more jobs for blacks on their films. He did not want to be guilty of the same thing for which he had criticized Murphy. So he negotiated with the unions to be allowed to hire a certain number of black, nonunion crew members, who would subsequently be eligible for union membership if they proved themselves with their work on *Do the Right Thing*.

By the time those negotiations were completed, Lee had decided where he wanted to shoot his film—the block of Stuyvesant Street between Lexington and Quincy Avenues in the Bedford-Stuyvesant section of Brooklyn. The only trouble with the block was that it harbored two busy crack houses, and Lee did not feel that his cast and crew would be safe with such businesses operating nearby. When the crew cleaned out the abandoned buildings that were used as location sites, they found empty M-16 rifle cartridges. All hours of the day, cars pulled up in front of the crack houses to buy drugs. Spike Lee could not shoot a film with all that going on.

He did not even consider bringing in the police to shut down the crack houses. He realized he would have to establish good relations with the people who lived on the block, and the police were not popular there. What he needed was a private security force of black men. Monty Ross had the idea of bringing in the Fruit of Islam, and they were hired as a security force at the beginning of set construction.

The Fruit of Islam are the self-defense arm of the Nation of Islam, sometimes called the Black Muslims. The most famous member of the Black Muslims was Malcolm X, who served as minister

Spike Lee's father, Bill Lee, with his bass. A musical purist,
he refused to make the transition to electronic music in the 1970s
and lost work as a result.

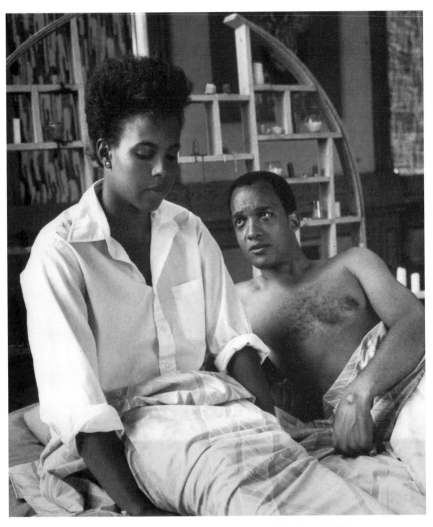

Tracy Camila Johns as Nola Darling and Redmond Hicks
as one of her three competing boyfriends in the "loving bed"
in Spike Lee's first film, *She's Gotta Have It*.

Spike Lee and his friend Monty Ross take a break during filming of *She's Gotta Have It.* In their college days in Atlanta, they shared their dreams about one day making films together.

Zimmie Shelton, Spike Lee's maternal grandmother.
After her daughter and Spike's mother, Jacquelyn Lee, died,
she provided both moral and financial support to help Spike realize
his dream of becoming a filmmaker.

Gamma Ray Jane Toussaint and Natural Rachel Meadows
in the "Straight and Nappy" number from *School Daze*.
In the film, the light-complected Gamma Rays and
the darker-skinned Naturals offer competing views
of what African-American women's identity should be.

Lee and cinematographer Ernest Dickerson (on the crane)
at work filming *School Daze*.
Critics consistently lauded Dickerson's work in Lee's films.

Spike Lee as Mookie, the pizza deliverer,
having a disagreement with his employer, Sal, played by Danny Aiello,
in *Do the Right Thing*.

The controversial riot scene in *Do the Right Thing,*
which some feared would inspire real-life riots
in racially tense urban neighborhoods.

Denzel Washington as Bleek Gilliam plays his horn on the Brooklyn Bridge, with the downtown Manhattan skyline as his backdrop in *Mo' Better Blues.*

In a tense scene in *Jungle Fever*, veteran actor Ossie Davis,
who plays the father of Flipper Purify (Wesley Snipes),
objects to Flipper's relationship with Angie (Annabella Sciorra),
while his on-screen and real-life wife, Ruby Dee, tries to calm him down.

Denzel Washington as Malcolm X in Spike Lee's epic film biography
of the charismatic leader.

Lee and Washington in Saudi Arabia,
where the scenes of Malcolm X's pilgrimage to Mecca were shot.

Alfre Woodard and Delroy Lindo as Carolyn and Woody Carmichael with their children at the dinner table in *Crooklyn*, Lee's most autobiographical film.

Lee with some of the young actors in *Crooklyn.* Like the Lee family, the Carmichael family includes four boys and one girl, Troy, played by Zelda Harris, through whose eyes the film is presented.

Mekhi Phifer as a drug dealer in the 1995 film *Clockers,* in which Spike Lee tried to treat the violence of the drug culture more seriously than he believed other films had done.

Spike Lee and Theresa Randle, star of *Girl 6*.

of Muslim Temple Number 7 in New York City and then national minister before becoming disenchanted with the Nation and leaving. In the 1980s Minister Louis Farrakhan also gained a national reputation. When Spike Lee's people made inquiries about hiring members of the Fruit of Islam, they were at first offered a force of one hundred men; but they decided twenty would do.

Like other Black Muslim men, the Fruit of Islam dress in suits, white shirts, and bow ties. They carry no guns, only walkie-talkies; but they are a force to be reckoned with. They had been successful in shutting down crack houses in many neighborhoods of Brooklyn and Queens, and they were prepared to do whatever was necessary to secure the block where Spike Lee was shooting his film. In no time, the two crack houses had been shut down, and there were no troubles after that. The police, of course, wanted to know who the black men in suits were, but Brent Owens, Lee's location manager, just said they were a private security force. He worried that the police might cause trouble if they knew that the security force on the *Do the Right Thing* shoot were members of the Fruit of Islam.

Working against deadline, Lee finished the second draft of the script on June 10. That same day he received the first $150,000 in start-up money from Universal. Principal casting had been completed by then. With cinematographer Ernest Dickerson and assistant director Lisa Jones, it was time to start planning the shots. In the middle of doing that, he flew out to Los Angeles to talk with the people at Universal about properly marketing the film. He did not want another marketing fiasco such as had happened with *School Daze*. In those weeks before shooting began, Spike Lee was like a juggler trying to keep a dozen balls in the air. One moment he was delegating someone to find pictures of Italian-American entertainers and athletes for the walls of the pizzeria; the next moment he was adding more dialogue to the script. He would confer with Ossie Davis and Ruby Dee about the money he could pay them and then take off for a meeting with the chairman of the film department at NYU about how to get more black students at the film school. He had agreed to set up a special minority student scholarship fund at NYU and to provide the first $5,000 scholarship. He had also set up a Forty Acres and a Mule film-training program at Long Island University. Having arranged with a junior high school near the film site to use the school as a holding area for the cast and crew, he agreed to give a speech to the students before the school year ended. He also established a scholarship fund at the school. From there he was off shopping for costumes. He was "crazy-busy," and he loved it.

While most filmmakers hold only one position—director or producer or set designer, for example—Spike Lee juggled many jobs at once. Part of the reason was money; he could save money by doing much of the work himself. But the bigger reason was that he wanted to control every aspect of his work. At times he was a one-man film production crew, not to mention one of the actors as well.

It bothered him that he had not had the time to focus on the character of Mookie, whom he would play; he felt Mookie was not quite fleshed out. Danny Aiello told him that he was a natural actor, but that he had "to get an activity." What he meant was that Lee needed to act with his body as well as with his face.

"Mookie has to have an activity," Lee wrote in his journal the next day. "Maybe he's always shuffling his feet. He has to do something. Another idea just came to me. Mookie might sound a bit

Italian—his intonations and the expressions he uses. He's worked at Sal's so long, it's rubbed off."[1]

Lee also learned from the other actors. John Turturro insisted on working with real pizzas, asserting that fake pies did not give the same feeling. Danny Aiello stood firm in his belief that the fight scene between himself and Giancarlo Esposito, who played Buggin' Out, was too slapdash as originally written. Esposito's father was Italian and his mother was black. During the filming, he and Aiello had become good friends and frequently spoke Italian to one another. As the two actors began to improvise in hopes of improving on the script, Aiello called Esposito a nigger. Esposito went wild and started calling Aiello every Italian epithet he could think of. Esposito was lashing back in pain. Later, he was upset with himself, as was Aiello. But Lee was delighted, because the real-life altercation had made his scene real. All the disagreements were eventually worked out, to the good of the film, Lee felt.

Shown a rough cut in December, Universal executives expressed concern about the ending and suggested alternatives, but Lee stood firm. He wanted the riot scene, and he wanted Mookie to be the one to start it by throwing a trash can through the window of the pizzeria. In the end, it was left the way he wanted it.

In its final form, *Do the Right Thing* was much as Spike Lee had first envisioned the film. It was visually striking, thanks to Ernest Dickerson's cinematography. Its score, written by Bill Lee and featuring the Branford Marsalis sextet backed by a forty-eight-piece string section, was the best for a Lee film yet. Although critics would say the movie did not have a strong plot, it had the most well-developed plot of any Spike Lee film to date. The main story line is about a pizzeria owned by a family of Italians—Sal and his sons,

Pino and Vito—that has remained open while the neighborhood has changed from Italian to black. Sal is proud of being in business in the same spot for so many years and believes he enjoys a generally good relationship with the people of the neighborhood. His older son, Pino, is ashamed of working in a pizzeria and hates the neighborhood. He tries to talk his father into selling out, but Sal will not hear of it. Sal does not consider himself a racist. He employs a neighborhood youth, Mookie, to deliver the pizzas; and he has a crush on Mookie's younger sister, Jade (played by Lee's real-life sister Joie). The people of the community generally like Sal and Vito, but they recognize the bald racism of Pino. They resent the pizzeria because it is white-owned in a neighborhood where there are few black-owned businesses. They are indignant that only pictures of Italian entertainers and athletes are displayed on the pizzeria's walls.

Mookie has a contentious relationship with the Italian family. He feels that Sal and Vito treat him well as a rule, but he recognizes their condescension in not allowing him to handle money or use the cash register. He points out to Pino that while Pino says he hates blacks, he is a big fan of black entertainers and athletes like Magic Johnson and Eddie Murphy. Mookie also has mixed feelings about his job, for while money is so important to him that he regularly counts and smooths his wad of cash, he frequently plays hooky from his job to visit his girlfriend, Tina, played by Rosie Perez. Tina and her little boy by Mookie live with her mother. Both women consider Mookie a n'er-do-well who has not taken proper responsibility for his child.

Mookie lives with his sister, Jade, who has a good job in a department store and wants to make something of her life. She, too, is always criticizing Mookie for his lack of responsibility. She is aware that Sal likes her and gently flirts with him.

As the day progresses and the heat grows more stifling, tensions among the people on the block increase. After kids on the block aim the water from a fire hydrant at a convertible being driven through the neighborhood by a white man, the man gets the police. The resulting confrontation between the police and the people on the block ends in the death of Radio Raheem, played by Bill Nunn, a neighborhood character who is never without his huge "ghetto blaster," which requires thirty batteries to operate and which is usually blasting a rap song called "Fight the Power." Furious, the people take out their anger on Sal's pizzeria. Mookie, who has not given much hint of militancy or political feeling before this time, is the one who starts the destruction of Sal's by throwing a trash can through its front window.

The next morning, the pizzeria is a burned-out shell. Sal arrives to inspect the damage. Mookie approaches and asks for his week's pay. Sal throws it down on the ground. "Do the right thing," he says. Mookie picks up the money, saying "I got it." As the film ends, two quotes appear in type on the screen. One, from Martin Luther King, Jr., is about violence: "Violence as a way of achieving racial justice is both impractical and immoral." The other is from Malcolm X: "When violence occurs in the instance of self-defense . . . I call it intelligence."

The audience is left to wonder what it all means. Why did Mookie, a generally sympathetic character, but with deep flaws, start the riot? Will Sal rebuild his pizza parlor? Have the people of the community destroyed a neighborhood institution for good? Who was right and who was wrong?

It is difficult to assign blame. The whites and the blacks have strong reasons for feeling and acting as they do. Spike Lee has given his audience no easy answers, leaving them to decide for themselves what the film means.

"The beauty of the film," Spike Lee told an interviewer for *Vogue*, "is that everybody's right. And everybody's wrong. And nobody's a hero."[2]

There was much in the film for audiences to think about. In *Do the Right Thing*, various characters of different races address the camera directly, spewing forth a stream of invective against another racial group: Mookie against Italians; Pino against blacks; Stevie, a Puerto Rican, against Koreans; a white police officer against Puerto Ricans; the Korean grocery store owner against Jews. This was a technique—having characters speak directly to the camera—that Lee had used in all his films.

Another was his use of minimusical essays, such as Mister Señor Love Daddy's roll call of black musical greats. Some critics said that particular minimusical essay was unnecessary. Others understood that it was one of the touches that defined a Spike Lee film.

In May 1989 Lee took *Do the Right Thing* to the Cannes Film Festival, where three years earlier he had stolen the show with *She's Gotta Have It* and walked off with the prestigious prize for best young director. Back then, he had shared a cramped apartment in the French resort with seven other people. This time he had his own two-room suite at the Carlton Hotel and was able to pay for members of his family to go to Cannes, too. This time, his photograph was up on a billboard alongside those of white directors Woody Allen and Francis Ford Coppola. Usually dressed in a T-shirt bearing the legend "Malcolm X: No Sellout," he could be seen at press conferences and parties talking up his new film. Since he thought *Do the Right Thing* was even better than his last, he had great hopes. But there is a politics to film prizes. Having won just three years earlier, he was unlikely to win again, no matter how good his film was. Instead, he was beaten out by twenty-six-year-old Steven Soderbergh and his film *sex, lies, and videotape.*

Nevertheless, Lee and his movie received a lot of press coverage, primarily, it seemed, because of its explosive ending and the concern of some that it might incite riots.

Critics would have a lot to say about *Do the Right Thing.* In fact, release of the film, the most controversial in many years, soon became less a cultural than a political event. One reason was that it was summertime, when, traditionally, racial riots occur. Another was that New York City was in the midst of a mayoral campaign in which a black man, David N. Dinkins, was a serious candidate.

In its July 3, 1989, issue *Newsweek* magazine presented the conflicting reactions side by side. In the first article Jack Kroll charged, "The real problem with 'Do the Right Thing' is that it's not radical enough. . . . In his attempt to be both ingratiating and militant, Lee has done the wrong thing." But in the second article David Ansen said, "You leave this movie stunned, challenged and drained. To accuse Lee of irresponsibility—of inciting violence—is to be blind to the movie he has made. The two quotes that end the film—Martin Luther King's eloquent antiviolent testament and Malcolm X's acknowledgment that violence in self-defense may be necessary—are the logical culmination of Lee's method. There can be no simple, tidy closure. Not now. Not yet. Lee's conscience-pricking movie is bracing and necessary: it's the funkiest and most informed view of racism an African filmmaker has given us."[3]

All the controversy only served to publicize the film, which grossed $18 million during its first month in spite of some stiff competition from other summer releases, including *Batman, Ghostbusters II,* and *Indiana Jones and the Last Crusade.*

To celebrate the success of *Do the Right Thing,* Lee contributed $50,000 to the United Negro College Fund and pledged to help raise $200,000 more. He also established a second $5,000 scholarship for minority students at NYU's film school.

That summer there were no riots and no incidents at movie theaters showing *Do the Right Thing.* In November, David Dinkins became the first black mayor of New York City. The following March, *Do the Right Thing* was noticeably absent from the spotlight at the annual Academy Awards.

The film had been extremely popular with critics. In fact, a 1990 *American Film* magazine poll of eighty newspaper, magazine, radio, and television film reviewers and critics revealed that they overwhelmingly preferred *Do the Right Thing* as the best picture of 1989 and Spike Lee as the best director. But the motion picture academy did not nominate either the director or the movie for an award. The film did receive two Academy Award nominations in lesser categories, but it failed to win any awards. Spike Lee wasn't surprised. He knew his film, and he, were too controversial to be accepted by the Hollywood establishment.

Although he had intended to make a controversial film, Lee was not prepared for the position in which he now found himself. Overnight, it seemed, he had been anointed as a militant black spokesman. He was besieged with requests to appear on television and radio talk shows to express his views on race relations. Although he was accustomed to being in front of a camera after appearing in all four of his movies, he had always played someone other than himself. He was not comfortable playing Spike Lee, spokesperson for the race. By nature a quiet person, he had always confounded newspaper and magazine interviewers by refusing to let down his guard. Now he was being asked to appear before cameras and bare his soul to an audience of millions. During one early television appearance, when asked to defend *Do the Right Thing*, he inexplicably went silent for a few agonizing moments. He never fully recovered his poise and wished he never had to appear on TV again. That night he called his grandmother in Atlanta and told her, "Mama, I just lost myself."[4]

Spike Lee would like to have withdrawn from the public eye. But he couldn't do it. Being a public person was part of the territory, part of a filmmaker's burden if he wanted to be a maker of controversial films; and especially part of a black filmmaker's burden if he wanted to be taken seriously. He never again found himself at a loss for words, but the statements he made began to sound canned, rehearsed, as if he had written a script for himself and decided to stick to it, keeping his real feelings and emotions to himself. His public statements were almost consistently militant and appeared also to be antiwhite.

In fact, Lee did resent whites for many things. He believed that a white director who had achieved his success would not have been forced to fight for what were still comparatively small budgets; would not have been asked why he hadn't yet treated the drug abuse theme in his films; would not have been charged with inciting urban unrest; would not have faced cancellations by theater owners because they feared his films might cause riots. Despite all these resentments, Lee was not antiwhite. Still, the remarks he made to soften the tone of his more militant statements were often lost in the stridency of his message.

What Lee hoped to do was use his position as a spokesperson to try to influence young blacks, whom he knew were not especially interested in Martin Luther King's philosophy of turn the other cheek and more likely to listen to the militant philosophy once preached by Malcolm X. But he found it difficult to get young people to see beyond the glamorous image they had of him as a successful, and rich, filmmaker.

Back in June 1989, just before the release of *Do the Right Thing*, Lee had spoken at Career Day at Boys and Girls High School, not far from where he had shot the film. "So how many of you think you might want to be filmmakers?" he asked the students. For a while there was no response. Then, just as the atmosphere began to get awkward, a girl piped up, "Can I be in your next film?" Everybody laughed, and then voices from around the auditorium cried out, "Yeah! Me, too!"

The response was not what Lee had wanted to hear. "I'm not here to lecture you," he said with a mixture of sadness and frustration. "But we have to start thinking about other career opportunities and less about being a star. We gotta change these values that tell us that success means having more gold chains than anybody else. Remember, no matter how much gold you have, you're still living where you're living, and not on the Upper East Side [the "gold coast" of Manhattan]."

He went on, "Look, without more black filmmakers, there aren't going to be any more black films. So if me, Eddie Murphy, and Robert Townsend are in a plane, and it crashes, you guys are in trouble, see? Next question!"[5]

6

Jazz and
Romance

Spike Lee was rich and famous, a
name in Hollywood. But he did not "go Hollywood." He had no
interest in huge houses with palm trees and swimming pools, in
celebrity parties, in the atmosphere of glamour and hype that he
was certain would destroy his concentration on making films about
the real black experience. He remained in his Brooklyn apartment,
in the world he knew, close to his family—although he could not
admit that was a factor. He had a telephone and a fax machine, and
he could keep in as close touch with Hollywood as he wanted, while
remaining a continent away. In choosing to stay in New York, he
was like another filmmaker, Woody Allen, whose creative well-
spring was New York and who could not imagine living anywhere
else.

It was reading about a planned Woody Allen film about jazz
that caused Spike Lee to decide on the subject of his next film. Lee
was very much his father's son in believing that jazz, a music origi-
nated by African-Americans, was *the* music and that no other musical style even compared to it. But he was sick of films about jazz as

seen through the eyes of whites. These films always seemed to portray black musicians as having instinctive talent, as if learning to play jazz wasn't hard work requiring years of study and practice. The musicians in these films always seemed to be addicted to dope, and their girlfriends were almost always white. Spike Lee believed that was a very one-sided depiction. In the fall of 1988 he decided to make a film about jazz that would be a realistic look into that world. As he wrote in his book about the film, "I was on a mission."[1]

Almost as soon as he had decided to do a film about jazz, Lee knew which actor he wanted to play the lead. Denzel Washington already had a long and distinguished career as an actor. Spike Lee wanted a star like Washington because his new movie was going to be his first in which there would be one major character rather than an ensemble of actors all playing roles of nearly equal importance. Moreover, Lee needed a lead character with a lot of sex appeal, for he had decided there was going to be a lot of romance in this film. He titled the film *Mo' Better Blues*. "The mo' better" is slang for lovemaking, and with that title Lee could refer to both music and the love story in the film.

Lee started making notes for the new film in December 1988. In January, his father had begun to set down ideas for the musical score. Lee decided to call the lead character Bleek (which was his father's nickname) Gilliam. One of Bleek's girlfriends would be named Indigo, and Joie Lee would play that role. The other woman would be named Clarke, for Lee liked traditionally male names for women. He had hoped to cast a brown-skinned woman in that role, so black women would not criticize him for pitting a light-skinned Clarke against brown-skinned Indigo. But he ended up choosing

Cynda Williams, even though she was biracial and very light-complected.

He knew he would cast himself in a role, and he started thinking about a character named Giant, a little guy, who was Bleek's friend from childhood as well as his manager, although not a very good one.

By April 1989, Lee had enough notes to write the first draft of his script. He was surprised at how easy it was to write, and yet he did not feel as strongly about it as he had about the first draft of *Do the Right Thing*. Compared to his earlier films, it was not very controversial. Would he be able to interest a movie studio in the script? Then he realized that it would be much easier to sell a conventional idea than the more controversial ones. He received positive reactions when he showed the script to the people at Universal. But he still didn't get the kind of money he wanted. So he sent copies of the script to other major studios as well.

Budget negotiations were long and drawn out, and in the end Universal came through with an offer he could accept. He got only $10 million when he had asked for $11.5 million, but $10 million was his largest budget to date, and he was not unhappy. With that kind of money, he could give his cast and crew a well-deserved raise, and he could shoot for ten weeks.

With his budget set and his contract with Universal Pictures signed, Lee gave the go-ahead for casting to take place. He offered a number of parts to actors with whom he had worked before: Ossie Davis, who took the role of Big Stop, Bleek's father, had appeared in *Do the Right Thing*; Giancarlo Esposito and Bill Nunn, who played members of Bleek's jazz group, had both worked in *School Daze* and

Do the Right Thing. Also from *Do the Right Thing* was John Turturro, who with his brother Nicholas played Moe and Josh Flatbush, the two brothers who own the club in which Bleek's group plays. Tracy Camila Johns and John Canada Terrell, from *She's Gotta Have It*, had bit parts as club patrons, as did Bill Lee, in the role of Indigo's father.

Monty Ross had a small part, and he again served as coproducer. Wynn Thomas, in charge of production design, Robi Reed, in charge of casting, and Ruth Carter, in charge of costume design, had worked with Lee in the past. Ernest Dickerson was again the cinematographer and David Lee the still photographer. All but two of the department heads were black. Of the dozens of other crew members, the majority were African-American, and there were seventeen interns who would be learning the techniques of film production.

Denzel Washington had some adjusting to do to Lee's directorial style and to the atmosphere on the set. He had never before worked with so many black people, both behind and in front of the cameras, and he was uncomfortable at first with the casual, friendly manner in which people related to one another. Washington was used to going off by himself and concentrating on his character. But, as he told Thulani Davis in an interview for the August 1990 issue of *American Film* magazine, he risked being seen as aloof. The attitude of the others was, "Wait a minute, don't even try it, don't even try walking by me this morning like you can't talk!" Washington went on, "The relaxed atmosphere was a wonderful thing but, because of it, it was more difficult concentration-wise."[2]

Also affecting Washington's concentration was his need to leave the set nearly every day and do promotion for his new film

Glory, which opened in theaters just as shooting on *Mo' Better Blues* was ending.

Despite these difficulties, Washington enjoyed working with Spike Lee, whom he described to Thulani Davis as "more quiet than most directors I've worked with." He explained, "We communicated, but there wasn't a lot of theater-type directing going on. He's more on the technical side of it. He expects you to come in and hit it. But he'll leave the camera on to allow things to happen. We would set up shots some time where he'd just set the camera up and say, 'OK, start talking.' In that regard, there was a lot more freedom to be spontaneous. He might just leave the camera on and see. So you got used to knowing that that was what was going to happen in certain circumstances. So you freed [sic] up that way. And probably some of the most interesting and funny stuff comes out of those times. He's mischievous. He likes to stir things up."[3]

As finally scripted, and improvised, *Mo' Better Blues* is the story of a musician who is devoted to his trumpet and who has little passion left over for the two women in his life. Music is of paramount importance to him, and to play his music he allows himself to be exploited by the Flatbush brothers, the owners of the club, Beneath the Underdog. His second greatest loyalty is to his childhood friend Giant, who is a lousy manager and also untrustworthy, since he is a gambler who cannot control his habit. In the most tragic sequence in the film, Giant gets himself into trouble over gambling debts and is beaten up, as is Bleek, who tries to rescue him. Bleek's lip is so badly cut that he can no longer play his trumpet. He must give up music, and when he does, he is forced to really see the two women who love him. He chooses Indigo, the schoolteacher, over Clarke, the aspiring singer. He and Indigo get married and have a child, and in the end the little boy is shown playing a trumpet, as his father did as a child before him. It is a film about relationships, Spike Lee explained to Lynn Norment of *Ebony*. "It's not only about man-woman relationships but relationships in general—Bleek's relationship with his father and his manager, and his relationship with two female friends. Bleek's true love is music, and he is trying to find the right balance."[4]

Spike Lee was pleased with the film, although he did not think *Mo' Better Blues* was as important a film as *Do the Right Thing*. Released in early August 1990, the film did not generate the controversy of its predecessor, nor did it do as well at the box office, although it did well for a jazz film. But there is always some controversy surrounding a Spike Lee movie. As Lee had expected, some black women criticized *Mo' Better Blues* because he had pitted a brown-skinned woman against a light-skinned woman, even though Indigo got Bleek in the end. What Lee had not expected were the charges of anti-Semitism leveled against him because of the portrayal in the film of the Jewish club-owner brothers as exploitive. He countered that the Flatbush brothers were not meant to represent all Jews any more than a character like Giant was meant to represent all blacks. His critics, however, were not satisfied.

Lee shrugged off the criticism. He was too busy promoting his movie and being involved in many other activities. That summer he opened Spike's Joint in a renovated brownstone in Fort Greene. His informal mail-order operation selling T-shirts and Brooklyn Dodgers baseball caps had mushroomed into a business that sold $50,000 worth of merchandise every month. After customers had started showing up at the mail-order office looking for merchandise, he decided to open a shop. Following his habit of keeping his business in the family, Spike hired his brother Chris to manage his store. Spike's Joint soon became a tourist attraction.

He was also doing a whole ad campaign for Levi Strauss and was still directing and appearing in ads for Nike. Few movie directors had been able to make the transition to commercial direction, as Spike had. He was in demand to appear in commercials and was hailed in the ad business as the first black "pitchman," as spokespersons are called in the ad business, whose appeal was based on a celebration of his color. A star like Bill Cosby succeeded as a marketer in spite of being black; Spike Lee succeeded because of it. His films were one reason. Another was that the public persona he had adopted had been accepted as authentic by the general public.

By the time *Mo' Better Blues* was released, Spike Lee was hard at work on his next film, *Jungle Fever*, which, like *Do the Right Thing*, was inspired by a racial incident. One evening in the summer of 1989, Yusuf Hawkins, a black youth, and three of his friends decided to go to the Bensonhurst section of Brooklyn to look at a used car they had seen advertised. They had no way of knowing that on the same evening some of the young men in the working-class Italian section were on the lookout for blacks coming into their neighborhood. A local girl had bragged that she had invited some of her black friends to her birthday party. She had previously been the girlfriend of one of the young white men. He and his friends were lying in wait for the blacks.

Yusuf Hawkins and his friends were surrounded by a crowd of menacing young whites. A shot rang out. Hawkins fell to the sidewalk, dead. The murder caused a furor in New York. The Reverend Al Sharpton led blacks in marches through Bensonhurst to protest the racism there. The marchers were taunted by crowds of young white men shouting racial epithets and holding up watermelons. Several young men were arrested and charged with the killing of Hawkins. Although some were found guilty of aggravated assault, none was convicted of murder.

In ghetto slang, the desire on the part of a white woman for a black man is called "jungle fever," and that is what Spike Lee decided to make his next film about. Interracial relationships were another taboo that movies rarely treated. Lee loved to make movies on subjects that no one else would touch.

Although executives at Universal Pictures were leery of Lee's subject matter, they backed him again and, based on the profits for *Mo' Better Blues*, gave him $14 million, a larger budget than for the previous film. Although Lee had hoped for an even larger budget, he realized that he was not going to get more than that as long as he insisted on complete control of his films. Universal Pictures head Tom Pollack, in speaking to Geri Hirshey of *Vanity Fair*, referred to that insistence indirectly when he cited Lee's troubling dislike of happy endings: "By and large, people go to the movies to escape from their trouble, get into *stories*, mythologies, reassurance. That's not what Spike Lee is about." Universal was not looking for Spike Lee to make a blockbuster film: "He makes good movies, and if they're done inexpensively, they're profitable. . . . When you make movies with Spike you aren't going for the home run."[5]

Midway through the writing of the draft script, Lee found even more reason to need a larger budget: He decided to include another plot dealing with the subject of drug use. Critics had charged that he had never treated the subject of drugs in his movies even though the drug culture was such an important, if tragic, part of inner-city black life. Lee decided that drugs and how they ruined lives could be a subplot in *Jungle Fever*.

Wesley Snipes was cast in the role of Flipper Purify. He had played the character of Shadow, who competes with Bleek Gilliam in music and for Clarke, in *Mo' Better Blues* and was then shooting *New Jack City*, a film by Mario Van Peebles. Flipper Purify is a successful architect who lives in a fancy section of Harlem called Striver's Row with a very light-complected wife, Drew, played by Lonette McKee, and their ten-year-old daughter. Ossie Davis and Ruby Dee played Flipper's parents, and Samuel L. Jackson took the role of Gator, Flipper's older brother, who is a crack addict. Spike Lee played Flipper's best friend Cyrus, and Veronica Webb, a model whom Lee was dating at the time, was cast as Cyrus's wife.

For the role of Flipper's secretary, Angie Tucci, who comes from a working-class family in Bensonhurst, Brooklyn, Annabella Sciorra was chosen. A "dark Italian," she is actually darker complected than Flipper's wife, a deliberate play on color prejudice. John Turturro plays her boyfriend, Paulie Carbone. Lee admired the work of the director Martin Scorsese, and he asked Scorsese's parents to play minor roles in the film.

Joie Lee did not appear in this film. Although Spike offered her a small role, she turned it down, explaining that she wanted to establish her own identity. Bill Lee wrote only two songs for *Jungle Fever*, much less participation in a movie of his son's than previously. Although both men refused to discuss the reasons why, saying only that they had mutually agreed to a time out from working together, it is likely that Bill Lee objected to his son's stereotyping of the interracial relationship in his film. He may have felt, and rightly so, that Spike's insistence that a black man and a white woman could not possibly love each other was a reflection of his feelings about his father's marriage to Susan Kaplan Lee. Stevie Wonder wrote the sound track for the film.

In the film, Flipper and Angie have an affair, with disastrous consequences. Angie's father throws her out of the house when he learns about it. Drew throws Flipper's things out onto the street when she learns he has been unfaithful. Angie breaks off the affair with Flipper, and he and Cyrus take a dangerous trip to Bensonhurst to find her. There, they are met by Angie's brothers and their friends and narrowly escape death when Cyrus, who like Lee himself doesn't have a driver's license, manages to make a mad drive to safety.

In choosing to set part of his story in Bensonhurst, Lee was taking a risk. The murder of Yusuf Hawkins and the events that followed had not changed the minds of many in that community about race. In fact, the controversy had solidified hatred of blacks among some residents. But when Spike Lee and his production manager walked through Bensonhurst to scout locations, Lee found proof of something he had written in *Do the Right Thing:* Just as the racist Pino had his black heroes and insisted they were "different," so Spike Lee found that the whites of Bensonhurst recognized and welcomed him, and asked for his autograph.

Filming took place in the fall of 1990, and by winter it was time for postproduction. Each film he had released so far had coincided with the release of a book about the making of the film. But as demands for his time had increased, he had found less and less opportunity to keep a log of how his films developed. His Day Runner datebook, with each day marked off into fifteen-minute segments, was so full of ink that he could not fit anything more into it.

So he did not write a book specifically about *Jungle Fever*. Instead, he produced *Five for Five*, in which he asked noted writers to do essays about the five films he had done so far. Liberally illustrated with photographs by David Lee, the book contained only an introduction by Spike himself.

Lee simply had too many other commitments to write a book for *Jungle Fever*. He was in constant demand as a speaker at high schools and colleges and as a TV spokesman for black Americans. Offers to direct came in droves. He declined an offer to design an ad campaign for Burger King. He was asked to direct a film of *Parting the Waters*, a biography of Martin Luther King, Jr., by Taylor Branch. He declined that offer, too. He was in the midst of writing the screenplay for a film about Malcolm X, and although he respected King and what he had done, he wanted to concentrate on the life of the late militant leader. Besides, he was just too busy.

He was in the process of expanding the line of Spike Lee clothing, films, and memorabilia at Spike's Joint, his retail store. He had signed his own record-production deal with Sony and was in the process of producing the sound-track album for *Jungle Fever*. He was directing an ad campaign for Diet Coke. He had shot a short feature on the boxer Mike Tyson for HBO. He was teaching a film workshop at Long Island University and had accepted an invitation from Harvard University to teach a film course there in the spring of 1992.

In the spring of 1991 he bought a three-story firehouse at 75 South Elliot Place in Fort Greene, not far from his apartment and about a mile from his father's house. After much renovation work, Lee moved his Forty Acres and a Mule Filmworks operation there, where he also set up a screening room and a T-shirt print shop. But he did not take on many other trappings of success. He still did not own a home. And he still did not have either a car or a driver's license.

Lee took *Jungle Fever* to the Cannes Film Festival in May 1991 and was pleased when Samuel L. Jackson earned the prize for best supporting actor for his role as Gator. He was not pleased that the film itself won nothing. Once again, he charged racism.

Dedicated to Yusuf Hawkins, *Jungle Fever* was released later in the summer in the United States and immediately ran into an unforeseen problem. Mario Van Peebles's film *New Jack City*, about black drug gangsters, had opened to big box-office sales—$10 million in the first week alone. But there had been riots in some of the big-city theaters where it was showing. In Los Angeles, rival gang members had engaged in a shootout. Just before the release of *Jungle Fever*, theater owners who had agreed to book the film called Universal to express fears that it would prompt more riots. Spike Lee was furious. A youth had been murdered during a showing of *Godfather, Part III* on Long Island, he pointed out, and no one had considered calling a halt to showings of that film. No one had blamed Francis Ford Coppola. No riots occurred at theaters where *Jungle Fever* was screened.

Just as Lee had expected, the film received considerable publicity because of its controversial subject matter. *Newsweek* devoted a cover story to *Jungle Fever*, and it was widely reviewed in other publications. Reviews were mixed. The film was criticized by many—black and white, men and women—for its one-dimensional depiction of black-white relationships.

Henry Louis Gates, Jr., a professor of English at Harvard University and head of the African Studies Department there, was a friend of Lee's and had invited him to teach a course at Harvard the following spring. But he was disturbed by what he identified as one underlying message of the film: Flipper Purify, successful and upper-middle-class, was a weak character who seemed to give up his blackness as he rose to success. This idea was in line with the current thought among blacks that "authentic" black culture was lower-class, ghetto culture. This attitude troubled Gates, as it did many other middle-class blacks. The attitude among too many ghetto youth was that to do well in school, for example, was to act "white." Faced with ostracism by their peers, more than a few bright students chose not to get good grades.

Although Lee had himself expressed concern over this attitude among young blacks, he had chosen to identify with it rather than to portray his middle-class black character in a positive light. His main point was that in having an affair with a white woman, Flipper Purify was betraying his race as well as himself. But he had also portrayed the very act of being middle-class as an example of betrayal.

Another element of black betrayal in the film was the drug subplot. Flipper's brother, partly in rebellion against their strict, Bible-quoting, ex-Baptist preacher father, sinks deeper and deeper into drugged despair. *Jungle Fever* was also praised for its depiction of how drugs can destroy lives and break up families. Ernest Dickerson, who had done a fine job on the film, earned special praise for the scene in which Flipper visits a crack house. Dickerson used color to underscore the chilling, life-threatening atmosphere, explaining later, "The crack house was all blue and green, which normally are the colors that are least flattering to black skin tone. But that was the point—to make it look like hell."[6]

In the opinion of many, Dickerson's work was what made the film. Wrote Armond White of the *City Sun,* "Unfortunately, Jungle Fever's visual sophistication is miles ahead of its verbalized and acted-out political ideas. In a sense, Dickerson's work is far too rich for Lee's simplified demonstration of what Black and white people, men and women, don't know about each other. He's photographing real people while Lee is using stick figures to dramatize a scheme."[7]

While *Jungle Fever* was no blockbuster, it did not lose money. The film industry did not look at Spike Lee's films individually, but rather at the body of his work. Every film he had made had turned a profit, and when there were profits people sat up and took notice. Also, Lee had turned out five films in the space of five years, enormous productiveness by Hollywood standards. He was credited with almost single-handedly reviving black films in Hollywood. In 1990–91 thirteen black-directed or -produced films had been released, more than in the entire previous decade. They included, in addition to Mario Van Peebles's *New Jack City,* John Singleton's *Boyz N the Hood* and Matty Rich's *Straight Out of Brooklyn.* Wrote Richard Corliss in *Time,* "One man created the market for black-movie rage: Spike Lee. . . . Lee, 34, has carved a niche for fierce minority movies—a niche that can be enlarged by other directors who are even younger, more choleric, closer to the action if not to the edge. Call them Spikettes."[8]

The other directors, including Mario Van Peebles, whose father, Melvin, led a similar breakthrough twenty years earlier with *Sweet Sweetback's Baadasssss Song,* credited Spike Lee with the breakthrough, but Lee himself pointed out that this rash of black films was not comparable to that which followed the Melvin Van Peebles film.

Jazz and Romance

Many of the blaxploitation films of the 1970s had featured blacks in front of the camera but not behind them. The 1990s films were directed and/or produced by blacks. Would this latest black Hollywood renaissance burn out as the last had? Lee was realistic. It all had to do with money. "All these films mean is that Hollywood can make a dollar off of them," he told *Time* magazine. "Black films will be made as long as they make money."[9]

7

Spike Lee's Home Run

Making money was only one of the reasons that Spike Lee's next film, *Malcolm X*, was so important to him. He wanted to do no less than to give young African-Americans a hero, a man who had been dead for nearly thirty years but who, Lee felt, could speak to the disaffected black youth in a way that no other leader, living or dead, could.

Spike Lee was only eight years old when Malcolm X was assassinated at the Audubon Ballroom in Harlem in February 1965, but he learned from his parents that a great man had been lost. He was eleven when Martin Luther King, Jr., was assassinated, and he heard again that a great man had been lost. In succeeding years, he heard much praise and criticism of both men, and he concluded, as he did at the end of *Do the Right Thing*, that each had been after the same goal: equality for black people. But their backgrounds and experiences led them on different paths in the fight for that equality.

Spike Lee had first read *The Autobiography of Malcolm X*, written with Alex Haley and published shortly after Malcolm's death, in junior high school. "It changed my life," he said years later. "To me, the veil was lifted. I no longer saw America through the eyes of a naive young black man."[1] He had considered Malcolm X a hero for years and had inserted references to the man wherever possible in his films. In *She's Gotta Have It*, Nola Darling had a giant poster of Malcolm X in her apartment. When Lee was having trouble raising money for that film, he had written in his journal, quoting Malcolm, that he would get the film made at all costs, "by any means necessary." That phrase also appeared on the cover sheet of his screenplay.

Once he had gotten to know Ossie Davis, who had known Malcolm well and had even delivered the eulogy at his funeral, Lee had often asked Davis to recall his days with the slain leader. In *Do the Right Thing*, the character Smiley goes around selling pictures of Martin Luther King, Jr., and Malcolm X, and there is an underlying point-counterpoint in the film between King's nonviolent philosophy and Malcolm's by-any-means-necessary one. The last frame of the film shows one of Smiley's pictures of Malcolm X being consumed by the fire in the pizza shop.

Spike Lee was not the only artist who was inserting references to Malcolm X in his works. More obvious were the lyrics of such rap and hip hop artists as Chuck D., with Public Enemy, and K.R.S.-One, with Boogie Down Productions. Beginning around 1990, when the twenty-fifth anniversary of Malcolm's assassination caused many blacks to begin reassessing his importance, they had started using Malcolm X's words in their songs, exposing a whole new generation to who he was. Many young people had never heard of Malcolm X. In fact, when some saw his name in print, they thought he was someone named Malcolm 10. Spike Lee gave these rap and hip hop artists full credit for beginning the revitalization of Malcolm X. He just started to build on what was already happening.

A film biography of Malcolm X was already in the works in Hollywood, and had been for close to twenty years. Malcolm X was a highly controversial figure and Hollywood is not usually comfortable with controversy. Over the years, there had been problems with scripts and over who would direct the film. In late 1990, Lee began lobbying Warner Bros., which owned the rights to the autobiography, to direct the film.

Lee believed that the real message of Malcolm X's life was personal growth. He had been an illiterate criminal, and he had educated himself while in prison. He had been a militant black nationalist, and he had learned that in the larger world the issue of racism was not as simple as he had formerly believed. Lee wanted to show this growth through film, and in so doing he wanted to send young black youth the message, as Malcolm X had tried to do, that education and personal growth were the real point of the life of Malcolm X. He also believed that only a black director could deliver that message to black youth.

Eventually, Lee persuaded the executives at Warner Bros. that his vision was the best and that he was the best director for the film biography of Malcolm X. He got the job and a budget of $28 million. He immediately began sporting a baseball cap with a picture of Malcolm and a large *X* on it.

Aware that this project was his most controversial to date, Spike Lee made sure to get the support of key people. He secured the cooperation of Malcolm's sister Yvonne, and brothers Wilfred, Omar, and Robert. He visited Malcolm X's widow, Betty Shabazz, who agreed to act as a consultant on the film. She was concerned about the picture Lee would paint of the Nation of Islam. She did not like Minister Louis Farrakhan, leader of the Nation of Islam, and believed his faction of the Nation had been responsible for her late husband's death.

Lee also visited Minister Farrakhan, whose Fruit of Islam had provided security on the set of *Do the Right Thing.* Lee wanted Farrakhan's assurance that his faction of the Nation would not try to disrupt or interfere with his film. Farrakhan gave the blessings of the Nation to the project. His major concern was how Lee would portray Elijah Muhammad, leader of the Nation of Islam until his death in 1976 and a one-time mentor of Malcolm's and Farrakhan's.

As was his habit, Lee made copious notes about scenes, not very many about characters, and who might play them. Denzel Washington had been signed to play the title role even before Lee had become involved, and *Malcolm X* would be very much Denzel Washington's movie. The other characters would be minor. For the first time, Lee did not try to think of a way to get members of his family involved. He had decided to give the family togetherness tradition in his films a rest.

There would, however, be a part for himself—in the role of Shorty, Malcolm's best friend in his petty criminal days. Although he would be busy behind the cameras, he believed he had a tradition to uphold by appearing in at least a minor role in the film. Many of the same members of his usual production team would be with him: Monty Ross as coproducer, Wynn Thomas as production designer, and of course Ernest Dickerson as cinematographer. They were a smoothly operating team by this time. Lee did not anticipate any problems in that area.

The major problems Lee had were with the script. It was very difficult to fit an entire life into a movie. Even though Malcolm X's life had been short—he died when he was forty—he lived many lives in his forty years. It was necessary to change events, to change names, to make three or four characters into one. Lee had no problem with doing that, for he was making a drama, not a documentary. The problem was *how* to do it. It took months of writing and rewriting to achieve an acceptable script.

Shooting began in September 1991, much of it on the streets of Harlem. Anticipating demonstrations against the project by individuals and groups who thought Lee would dilute the late leader's story to make it more acceptable to whites and middle-class blacks, Lee decided to hire the Fruit of Islam as a security force on the shoot. Lee also paid members of the Nation as consultants to give Denzel Washington a two-week training course in the principles and practices of the Nation. Both Lee and Washington had decided that this was crucial to his learning about what made Malcolm X tick.

Once shooting began, Washington became lost in his role, and those around him knew enough not to interrupt his concentration. Having worked together before, he and Lee understood each other's moods and methods. Both were aware that their reputations were riding on this film.

The outside world intruded on Spike Lee that fall in spite of all his efforts to keep focused on his Malcolm X project. In October his father was arrested for possession of a small amount of heroin. Although Bill Lee had used drugs recreationally for as long as Spike Lee could remember, this was the first time he'd been caught. Given probation, for it was his first offense, Bill Lee apparently toed the line after that. Their father's arrest brought the Lee children together for a time, but it did nothing to heal the rift between Spike and his dad.

The job of editing the thousands of feet of film he had shot still lay ahead for Spike Lee. He believed that the larger-than-life Malcolm X required a longer-than-usual film. But editing a three-hour film takes more time and thus costs more money than the standard two-hour film. Already over budget, Lee was not about to be stymied at this critical stage. He sought outright gifts of money from wealthy black stars to complete his film, and they gave him the money. Lee understood that this was a rare occasion of black solidarity, and in May 1992 he held a special press conference at the Schomburg Center for Research in Black Culture in Harlem to give public thanks to his special donors. He also used the occasion to dispel rumors that the film was in trouble because Warner Bros. was not behind it. Company executives had seen a four-hour version of the film twice, said Lee, and were fully behind it.

There was still much to do to get the film down to a more manageable length, which finally was three hours and twenty-one minutes. That process was going on in April when large riots occurred in Los Angeles. Sparked by the acquittal of white Los Angeles police officers charged in the near-fatal beating of black motorist Rodney King on March 3, 1991, large sections of south-central Los Angeles exploded in fury.

In Lee's opinion, his film about Malcolm X could not be more timely. There was a rage in the inner cities that was similar to that of the early 1960s, when Malcolm X was at the height of his influence. Lee decided to use footage of the Rodney King beating in the opening of his film.

As the date for the opening of the film *Malcolm X* neared,

tensions increased for Spike Lee. Some of the tensions were of his own making. He announced that the opening of the film on November 20 was such a historic event that young people should skip school and go see it. This announcement touched off a storm of criticism from people who said that Malcolm X had so valued education that he would not approve of anyone's skipping school to go and see a film about him.

The media attention was enormous. Lee had helped to create a phenomenon that even he could not control. He was besieged by reporters seeking interviews, and some of them were hostile. Lee decided it was time to protect himself from the press even more than before. Four weeks before the scheduled premiere of *Malcolm X*, he announced that henceforth he would prefer to be interviewed by African-Americans.

He was hardly the first media personality to attempt to control access to himself. Movie stars have done so for years. He insisted that he was doing nothing more than white media stars did. Moreover, he pointed out that if there were more black reporters he wouldn't have the problems he had with so many white interviewers. Not that black writers did not ask him tough questions. But he felt that on the subject of Malcolm X black writers would approach the interviews with a greater degree of understanding, both spiritually and intellectually.

The New York premiere of *Malcolm X* on November 18, 1992, was attended by a gala crowd that included Betty Shabazz and her six daughters. Two days later, the film opened in 1,100 theaters across the country, to headlines in most major newspapers, and to raves from critics. Spike Lee had staked his reputation on *Malcolm X*, and his gamble had paid off.

The opening of the film promises controversy, with its footage of the beating of Rodney King by Los Angeles police officers and a burning American flag whose charred remains reconfigure as the letter X. But what follows is a sober look at the life of Malcolm X with very few inflammatory scenes or other efforts to provoke controversy. In fact, Spike Lee generally played it straight with the story of Malcolm X, letting the man's life speak for itself.

The film portrays the life of Malcolm X (born Malcolm Little) in three one-hour acts, each phase colored differently by cinematographer Ernest Dickerson. The first hour of the film presents his early life primarily through flashbacks and is chiefly devoted to Malcolm's life on the streets of Boston and New York in the 1940s. Lee and Dickerson tried to make the film look like a 1940s movie, using filters and even placing stockings over lenses to give the scenes warmth. This style tended to obscure the seriousness of Malcolm's early criminal life—his pimping and drug taking. Partly, this was a marketing move. Malcolm X in those years was a rough, uneducated criminal; but to have portrayed that period of his life realistically would have jeopardized the PG-13 rating that Spike knew the film would need in order to be successful.

It is in this section that Malcolm meets his friend Shorty, played by Spike Lee, and there is considerable humor in their relationship, which also tends to gloss over the fact that both were criminals. Although in the film it is Shorty who introduces Malcolm to a life of crime, in real life it was the other way around. The point is clearly made in the film, however, that in those days, with his processed hair and his life of crime, Malcolm was degrading himself.

Imprisoned on a burglary charge, Malcolm takes a sober look at his life. The tone and look of the film turn sober as well, the cinematography stark and cold. For dramatic purposes, Lee has a fellow inmate preach to Malcolm about the Nation of Islam, when in actuality it was members of his own family who converted him.

The third hour-plus covers Malcolm's years in the limelight as Minister Malcolm X. It treats the Nation of Islam and its black separatist teachings seriously, and there are no cinematographic gimmicks. It is equally serious in its treatment of Malcolm's split with the Nation. For Malcolm's pilgrimage to Mecca, Dickerson again used filters, softening the visual effect and emphasizing the importance of the pilgrimage to Malcolm's life. Malcolm X's assassination is portrayed as a conspiracy between the Nation of Islam and the Federal Bureau of Investigation. His death is presented as a tragic loss for black America. Over newsreel footage of Malcolm's funeral, Ossie Davis reads the eulogy that he actually read at the funeral: "Malcolm was our shining prince. He represented what's best in us, what we can be, our black manhood."

The closing sequence shows the black nationalist Nelson Mandela quoting Malcolm X to black schoolchildren in South Africa, which in 1992 had not yet ended its system of apartheid, rigid racial separation. The message of that closing sequence, as well as of the opening sequence, was that what Malcolm X fought against more than a quarter century earlier still existed, but that the spirit of resistance that Malcolm X embodied was still there, too.

"We make the connection between Soweto and Harlem, Nelson and Malcolm, and what Malcolm talked about—pan-Africanism, trying to build these bridges between people of color," Lee explained. "He is alive in children in classrooms in Harlem, in classrooms in Soweto."[2]

The movie ends by encouraging viewers to read *The Autobiography of Malcolm X*. "We've got to turn this backward thinking around where ignorance is champion over intelligence," says Spike Lee. "Young black kids being ridiculed by their peers for getting A's and speaking proper English: that's criminal."[3]

Whether many blacks skipped work or school to see it, the large majority of audiences the first day—in some cases up to 80 percent—were black and young. They spent more than $2 million on tickets that day—far more than audiences had spent on the only recent film of comparable length, Oliver Stone's *JFK*. Most emerged from the theater feeling that their money, and their time, had been well spent.

Many critics thought that the film was too long. While most understood that Lee had feared diminishing Malcolm X by devoting any less time to him, they pointed out that he had thereby reduced the size of the audience that would see the film, for there were some people who simply would not sit through a film that long. Other critics suggested that this was one film in which Spike Lee should have remained behind the cameras, saying that he overemphasized the importance of the comparatively minor character Shorty. Critics felt that the opening sequence promised a provocativeness that the rest of the film failed to deliver. Nevertheless, most allowed that Lee, with the help of Denzel Washington, had indeed managed to bring Malcolm X to life again.

Vincent Canby of the *New York Times* praised Spike Lee for his restraint, for through his earlier films Lee had acquired a reputation as something of a showboater. Wrote Canby, "Mr. Lee's method is almost self-effacing. He never appears to stand between the material and the audience. He himself does not preach. There are no carefully inserted speeches designed to tell the audience what it should think. He lets Malcolm speak and act for himself. The moments of confrontational melodrama, something for which Mr. Lee has a particular gift, are quite consciously underplayed."[4]

And Denzel Washington received raves for his acting. Wrote Julie Salamon in the *Wall Street Journal,* "Mr. Washington resists the temptation to make Malcolm into something he never was. He doesn't demonize or sanctify, either by making him a wild-eyed firebreather or by cheating with false foreshadowing—by winking to the audience to let it know that the stern man who calls Martin Luther King an Uncle Tom and who denounces all whites will change. It's a wonderful performance, as mesmerizing for its subtlety as for its power."[5]

So thoroughly does Washington embody Malcolm X that when, toward the end of the picture, Lee introduces actual black-and-white film footage of the real Malcolm X giving a speech, it is a shock to realize that he doesn't look and sound exactly like the actor who portrays him.

The critical praise was just what was needed to make sure white audiences went to see *Malcolm X.* Soon full-page newspaper ads for the film appeared, carrying excerpts from the rave reviews. These ads were calculated to attract that larger audience to see the film.

Meanwhile, theaters had found a way to schedule showings of the film to get the maximum number of showings each day, just as they had managed to do with Oliver Stone's three-hour *JFK,* which had sold more than $70 million in tickets in the United States. At large, multiscreen theater complexes, the movie was being shown on up to three screens, with staggered starting times, so that it could be shown more than once a night in many communities.

The film helped spark a renaissance for Malcolm X. Video

documentaries played to packed audiences. CBS-TV aired an hour-long special called *Malcolm X: The Real Story*. Magazines and newspapers carried articles about him. Libraries could not keep books about Malcolm X on their shelves, and *The Autobiography of Malcolm X*, first published a quarter of a century earlier, was suddenly number one on the *New York Times'* paperback nonfiction list. Spike Lee may not have started "Malcolmania," but his film had helped it to coalesce.

"It couldn't be a good film, it had to be a great film," he told an interviewer for *New York* magazine. "We only come to the plate one time, and we have to hit a home run," Spike Lee had said in early September.[6] Well, he'd hit a grand-slam home run.

Malcolm X had grossed $2 million in box-office receipts its first day. But the number of tickets purchased for its initial run told only part of the story. Sales of the two-tape video version, which was released the following year, were brisk, as schools purchased it for classroom viewing and individuals bought it to view at their leisure at home. Although there are, by definition, no accurate figures for bootleg video sales, the fact that poor-quality bootleg versions were available literally hours after the film was released also attested to the film's popularity.

At long last, Spike Lee had proved to Hollywood—and the world—that a black filmmaker, more particularly, the filmmaker Spike Lee, could take a large budget and larger-than-life subject and make an epic film. He had taken a man who was not hugely popular in his lifetime and made him a hero for the 1990s. He had made a film that whites, as well as blacks, wanted to see.

It had taken years of fighting and working and taking the attitude "by any means necessary," but Spike Lee had won. Now he looked forward to the time when he could live a less hectic, normal life. He wanted to make more movies, and had lots of ideas, but he did not feel the need to make them one right after another, as he had earlier in his career. Six films in six years was a tremendous output, which had taken a heavy toll on him. He knew there was more to life than working and striving. He wanted to take time out for himself.

8

Ten-Year Veteran, with the Scars to Prove It

After publicizing *Malcolm X* in Europe in January, Lee planned to return to Harvard University in Cambridge, Massachusetts, in February to teach classes in contemporary African-American cinema and screenwriting. He'd taught classes at Harvard the previous winter and had enjoyed the chance to talk—and argue—with bright students.

Lee liked Massachusetts. He had bought his first home there, a house on Martha's Vineyard, and he was eager for the time when he would be able to escape to it, enjoy some much-needed privacy, and take a good long rest. He also looked forward to the time when he would get married and raise a family.

The ideal marriage, in Lee's eyes, was that of veteran actors Ossie Davis and Ruby Dee, who had met when they had appeared together in the play *Jeb* in 1946 and who had married two years later. Lee had also given some thought to how he wanted his children educated. They would go to New York City public schools, he had decided, so they would get a sense of the real world; he considered private schools too sheltered.

There were plenty of women interested in Spike Lee, but thus far none of his relationships had lasted. Then Spike Lee met Tonya Lynette Lewis.

A practicing attorney in Washington, D.C., Lewis met Lee in the early fall of 1992. They began dating immediately, and three months later Lee broached the subject of marriage. It was not his style to propose in romantic fashion. The two were vacationing in Antigua, and Lee suddenly said, "So when are we getting married?" Lewis, somewhat nonplussed, answered, "Why? Are you asking?" Lee responded, "That depends on what your answer is."[1] They were married the following October at Riverside Church in New York City.

Both Lee and Lewis were eager to start a family, and they wasted no time in doing so. Their first child, a daughter, was born in early December 1995. Lee took some ribbing about the fact that the baby was a girl, because he had once said publicly that he wanted only sons. His wife told him he'd cursed himself for saying that and would never have any sons. But Lee was hoping the next child might be a boy.

In the meantime, because he could not be sure he would have a son, Lee named his little girl Satchel, after the great Negro baseball league pitcher Satchel Paige. It just so happened that the white filmmaker Woody Allen had given the name Satchel to his son by actress Mia Farrow; but Spike Lee decided he had as much claim on the name as Allen.

Lee's focus on family during this time of his life translated to his next movie, *Crooklyn*, the story of a black lower-middle-class Brooklyn family in the early 1970s. In late September 1992, Lee had signed a multiyear deal with Universal Pictures that gave the studio a first look at all movie projects he developed. Lee had gone to Warner Bros. for *Malcolm X* because that studio owned the rights to the film. But he was happy to return to Universal, with which he'd had a relationship since *Do the Right Thing*. He had negotiated the contract from a position of great strength, thanks to *Malcolm X*. *Crooklyn* was his first film under that contract.

Crooklyn provided Lee with an opportunity to work with members of his family again. Written with the help of his sister, Joie, who plays a character named Aunt Maxine, and his brother Cinque, the screenplay is highly autobiographical. Like the Lee family, the Carmichael family lives in a brownstone, the children number four boys and one girl, the father is a musician who would rather stay true to his music than play with rock bands and earn a decent salary, the mother is fiercely determined to keep her children in school and out of trouble. Even some of the names are close to the real ones. The mother is named Carolyn (Lee's mother was named Jacquelyn); the little girl is named Troy (Lee's sister is Joie).

The film, Lee's first to appeal to children, is told through the eyes of Troy and is filled with realistic sequences about Troy's shoplifting, spending hours in front of the mirror willing her breasts to develop, and stealing her brother's coin collection to buy ice cream. It also portrays a black family untouched by drugs (although Lee plays a neighborhood glue sniffer), crime, or divorce. In fact, there are few strong dramatic elements to the story until close to the end, when a death in the family causes the other members to be strengthened by their loss.

The team that had made so many Spike Lee movies lost a key member when Ernest Dickerson decided to strike out on his own as a director. The absence of Dickerson's cinematography is very evident in *Crooklyn*, which was shot by Arthur Jafa, cinematographer of the hauntingly beautiful *Daughters of the Dust* by the black filmmaker Julie Dash. The overall look is bland, and the camera tricks are too evidently just that. In one part of the film, Troy is sent South to live with uptight relatives; the entire sequence is filmed through a distorting lens, which is supposed to produce a weird effect. It does, but not one the audience feels comfortable with. Rather than conveying Troy's feeling of being out of place dramatically, it imposes this point of view on the audience.

A clue to the modesty of the film was the timing of its release—May 1994—months away from the usual big-movie release times of just before Christmas and early summer. Its box-office receipts were also modest, with a gross of $13.6 million.

Lee's next film, *Clockers*, could not have been more different from *Crooklyn*. Based on the 1992 novel of the same name by Richard Price, the film was supposed to have been directed by Martin Scorsese. But Scorsese elected to direct another film, *Casino*. Offered Scorsese's place, Lee had strong misgivings about the project, which he called a "black gangsta, hip-hop, shoot-'em-up" story.[2]

In the novel, Richard Price gave equal time to the nineteen-year-old crack dealer, Strike, and to Rocco, a white homicide detective counting the days until his retirement. Robert De Niro was to have played the role of Rocco, almost guaranteeing that the white detective would be the central character in the film. Lee was not eager to direct a film with a white central character. But Robert De Niro chose to leave the project once Scorsese had done so. Although Lee had wanted to work with De Niro and had originally hoped to cast him in the role of Sal, the pizzeria owner in *Do the Right Thing*, De Niro's departure allowed Spike to see how he could make the film his own. In the end, he agreed to take over the project because it was an opportunity both to answer his critics and at last make a film about drugs and to treat the violence of the drug culture more seriously than he believed other films had done.

In his opinion, many recent films by blacks were too violent and little but throwbacks to the black exploitation films of the 1970s. He had even called for greater responsibility in depicting violence in films and videos. Although he accepted the *Clockers* project reluctantly, he realized the film was his opportunity to practice what he preached. But he hoped *Clockers* would be the last violent urban black film for a while. "It's dead! It's over! Move on!" he said, referring to the film type. "I loved *Boyz N the Hood* and *Menace II Society,* but those other films, I don't know. The genre is at its end now. It's up to African-American film makers to open our vision. If you don't expand and grow, you die."[3]

The term "clocker" is slang for a small-time drug dealer who hustles around the clock. Strike, played by Mekhi Phifer, already has an ulcer at the age of nineteen. He wants more than anything else to get off the streets. His boss, Rodney, played by Delroy Lindo, tells him that he can deal indoors if he proves himself trustworthy by killing another dealer.

Then the dealer turns up dead, and Strike finds himself caught between Rocco, played by veteran actor Harvey Keitel, the white detective who thinks he committed the murder, and Rodney, who doesn't believe he did. Strike is "C2D," slang for close to death.

Strike is living in hell. He is beaten by his mother for drug dealing, stomped by cops, terrorized by Rodney. By the end of the film, his ulcer has become perforated and he is spitting blood. Meanwhile, his world is an inferno of death. There are four fatal shootings, including a multiple execution. Death hovers, and lives are lived at a crescendo of fear.

Lee used many of his signature film techniques to portray the violence in the film as graphically as possible. The opening sequence of the film, which was released in September 1995, includes a montage of still photographs depicting young black males of all complexions lying dead of bullet and puncture wounds, re-creations of the goriest photographs available from the New York City Police Department's crime scene unit. Immediately following the credits comes another Lee signature technique, a "Greek chorus" of five teenage boys on benches in the middle of a high-rise housing project making irreverent hip-hop comments. A third Lee signature is to end his films with messages; in *Clockers*, there is a shot of a member of the Nation of Islam selling copies of the Nation's newspaper at a railway station, as if to suggest that joining the Nation is another way out of the ghetto.

A fourth Lee signature—his concern with neat and sanitized environments—proved to be unfortunate. The film includes perhaps the most graphic depiction of a crime scene to date: Police arrive to inspect the body of a murder victim, and they are shown probing bullet holes, inspecting brains spilling out of the skull, holding their noses because of the stench of feces. The scene, an early one in the film, is marked by physical and emotional force. But in most of the rest of the film there is an aura of unreality. Most of the drug users in the film are shown only as drug buyers. There is no drug litter, no crack vials, no used needles. *Clockers* was shot in the Gowanus Projects in Brooklyn, whose sidewalks and other common areas are in reality strewn with crack vials, syringes, even spent bullet shells. None of this litter is evident in Lee's *Clockers*, whose idealized environment recalls his *Crooklyn*. In fact, a newspaper headline in the film identifies the place as Crooklyn.

Except for *Malcolm X*, in which Lee was constrained by facts from imposing his own vision, all of his previous work had been expressions of his own experience. *Clockers* was another film in which he was challenged to tell a story that was not originally his own. In the opinion of most critics, although the film was largely successful, in the end he failed to meet that challenge.

The film did not do well at the box office, grossing just $13 million.

With the last two of his films for Universal having done poorly at the box office, Lee did not take his next film, *Girl 6*, to that studio. Instead, he approached Miramax. But then Miramax changed its mind and backed out. Lee had to shop *Girl 6* around for quite a while before signing a deal with Fox Searchlight Pictures, the art film division of 20th Century Fox.

The comparatively poor showing at the box office of Lee's recent films was only part of the problem with *Girl 6*. The other was its subject matter: An aspiring actress needs to pay the rent, and so she decides to take a job as a phone sex operator while she waits for her big break. In spite of the fact that the screenplay was written by playwright Suzan-Lori Parks, who had won an Obie in 1990 for her off-Broadway play *Imperceptible Mutabilities in the Third Kingdom*, and that Lee planned to have stars like Madonna and Halle Berry in cameo roles, many studios simply did not think the film would make money—and making money is what Hollywood filmmaking is all about. Nevertheless, Lee persevered, convinced that Hollywood needed more roles for black actresses. Besides, he was aware that his tenth anniversary as a professional filmmaker was approaching, and the echoes of his first film, *She's Gotta Have It*, in this film appealed to him.

Like *She's Gotta Have It*, *Girl 6* presents women who seem to have all the power and whose characters are the most fully realized. While the men who call the telephone sex line imagine the women feeling real emotion as they speak, the women are just mouthing words while they file their nails or work crossword puzzles. But the title character, played by Theresa Randle, wrestles with conflicting feelings about her job. She wants to be a real actress, and the acting she does on the other end of a telephone sex line is not what she has in mind at all. Of great concern to her—and to the audience—is that as time goes on she gets more and more involved in her role as telephone sex purveyor.

Theresa Randle, whose only other film had been the 1994 drug-racketeer drama *Sugar Hill*, had ample opportunities to show the range of her acting talents in the film. As Girl 6, she daydreams about becoming a star like Dorothy Dandridge, the beautiful but tragic black actress of the 1940s and 1950s, or perhaps doing TV comedy. Her impersonation of Dandridge in the 1954 film *Carmen Jones*, and her parody of the role of the maid in the TV sitcom *The Jeffersons*, are right on target. As one reviewer put it, she began the film as a starlet and ended up as a star.

Other actors in the film included Isaiah Washington from *Clockers* as Girl 6's ex-husband, the director Quentin Tarantino playing a director, John Turturro from *Do the Right Thing*, *Mo' Better Blues*, and *Jungle Fever*, as a sleazy agent, and Lee himself as Girl 6's neighbor, Jimmy, an avid collector of baseball memorabilia (Jimmy's collection in the film is actually Lee's own). Supermodel

Naomi Campbell played a cameo role as another phone sex operator, and Madonna appeared in another cameo as Boss 3, one of the bosses of the phone sex company.

The metaphor Suzan-Lori Parks chose for Girl 6's descent into the darker regions of the phone sex industry is that of a little girl falling down an elevator shaft. The film opens with this image—a just-breaking news story about an eight-year-old named Angela who has fallen down an elevator shaft. The incident captures the attention of the entire city, and Girl 6 is riveted by the daily news accounts of the little girl's recovery. Although she does not want to admit it to herself, she is falling, too.

As in earlier Spike Lee films, the sound track is crucial to the story. The driving beat of the music composed by the artist formerly known as Prince interweaves his classic songs with new compositions created especially for the film. Also as in earlier Lee films, the visual style created by cinematographer Malik Sayeed is stunning.

But the film lacked structure, and critics charged that despite clear efforts, Lee failed again to overcome one of his biggest problems—an inability to create a female character who is more than one-dimensional. Released on March 19, 1996, the film did not do especially well with movie audiences either.

When the annual Cannes Film Festival rolled around in May, Spike Lee was in attendance. In some ways, it was painful for him to be there. He remembered the years of *Do the Right Thing* and *Jungle Fever*, when he truly believed he had a winner and was sorely disappointed when he was shut out of major awards, losing, in some cases, to inferior films. This year, he wasn't even in competition—neither he nor *Girl 6* had been nominated in any category. But Lee had serious business to conduct in Cannes: He was selling *Girl 6* to foreign distributors. As in the case of most films, fully 50 percent of his films' box-office revenues had been generated internationally.

Older and wiser now about awards, he understood that the failure of any of his earlier films to win at Cannes had not hurt the films. He'd had to learn not to allow losing—or not even seeing his films nominated—to hurt him. As he told assembled reporters at a press conference, "I think you just set yourself up for a lot of heart-break if you allow any group, whether it be the jury in Cannes or the Academy of Motion Picture Arts and Sciences, to have the authority to say whether your work is worthwhile." He then added sarcastically, "Especially looking at the Academy Awards this year!" referring to the fact that of 166 individual nominees, only one was a member of a minority group.[4]

But Spike Lee's problems went deeper than his being a member of a minority group. As he marked his ten-year anniversary as a professional filmmaker, Spike Lee realized he was at a career crossroads. His recent films had been far from blockbusters. Any filmmaker of lesser movies who wished to remain a player in Hollywood either had to settle for a more modest niche as a filmmaker of lower-budget films with smaller audiences and stop pretending that a blockbuster was possible or had to come up with a blockbuster of his or her own.

Spike Lee had plumbed the depths of his own experience in seven of his nine professional films, and focused on the larger black experience in two others. He hoped to turn to a subject he loved, baseball, and use it to reflect the larger black experience, in a planned film biography of Jackie Robinson. Given American's love of baseball, the film biography of the first black player in the major leagues had the potential of being a big film. The target date for its opening was 1997, the fiftieth anniversary of Robinson's major league debut with the Brooklyn Dodgers; Lee planned to get Denzel Washington to play the starring role.

But Lee could not agree on a budget for the film with Turner Pictures, the motion picture division of Ted Turner's media empire. Lee wanted a budget of $35 million; Turner would not go higher than $25 million. If the film were to be made, it would be without Spike Lee.

"The same glass ceiling the African Americans face in corporate America—well that same ceiling exists in this industry," Lee said.[5] He was referring to the fact that there are no major African-American studio executives with the power to say "I want to make this movie" and have the movie made.

Spike Lee could have compromised. He could have agreed to the lower budget and made the film somehow. But he believed in himself and in the value of his project, so he didn't.

Instead, he turned right around and made another film, a modest film on a low budget that did not require a compromise. It was the perfect kind of film for him—a film that investigated the many facets of the African-American experience. *Get On the Bus* is a film about fifteen black men on a bus on their way to the Million Man March.

On October 16, 1995, hundreds of thousands of black men converged on Washington, D.C., in answer to the call of Minister Louis Farrakhan of the Nation of Islam. Farrakhan, along with civil rights leaders including the Reverend Jesse Jackson and the Reverend Benjamin Chavis, intended the march as a massive show of unity by black men, whom they considered the most "endangered species" in America. The Million Man March was an expression of atonement in which black men demonstrated their awareness that they were themselves responsible for much that afflicted their group, that they had not taken care of their families nor been good role models for their communities. At the same time, the Million Man March aimed to assert the positive potential for black political strength—a strength that could be marshalled in votes and political action against cutbacks in education, job-training, and other social-welfare programs.

The title, Million Man March, meant just what it indicated: women were not invited. In Farrakhan's view, and based on his adherence to the teachings of Elijah Muhammad, black men bore the chief responsibility for the black family, and thus for black life. Women's support was welcomed, but in a background capacity, such as raising money to pay for buses to transport men to the capital.

On the day of the march, the National Parks Service estimated the crowd at 400,000. March organizers insisted that they had exceeded their goal of one million. Whatever the number, it was huge—the largest group of black people ever to have converged on Washington, D.C. They wore suits and ties, workclothes and overalls, blue jeans and hooded sweatshirts. They were young and old, Christian and Muslim, professionals and laborers and the unemployed, and of every hue in the spectrum from light to dark. Many men brought their sons to share in the historic moment. Here and there, a few women could be spotted, in attendance to support black men. March organizers had planned for crowd control, and the Fruit of Islam were out in force. But in the entire day there was not a single incident of violence, or even unruliness. It was a happy crowd, a proud crowd.

Even for those who did not attend the march, and Spike Lee was among them, the event was a cathartic experience. Lee wanted to convey that experience on film, and so with a group of African-American investors (including actors Danny Glover and Wesley Snipes and attorney Johnnie L. Cochran, who had recently defended O. J. Simpson against criminal charges of murdering his former wife), he raised $2.4 million to make a film that would show the energy and shared commitment that had made the march such a huge success. Moreover, he determined to release the film in time for the one-year anniversary of the march in October 1996.

To make the movie, Lee had to recall his early days as a low-budget filmmaker, when he would make the most of whatever resources he had to work with. The strengths he had developed and the lessons he had learned over the years helped him as he gathered an ensemble of actors to represent the spectrum of African-American men, traveling on a bus called the Spotted Owl from Los Angeles, California, to the march in Washington, D.C. The characters include an absentee father (Thomas Jefferson Byrd) who is, under court order, literally linked by a chain to his petty criminal son (DeAundre Bonds); a gay couple (Isaiah Washington and Harry Lennix); a wise elderly man (Ossie Davis); a half-white man who also happens to be a policeman (Roger Guenver Smith); an actor with a huge ego (Andre Braugher); a practicing Muslim (Gabriel Casseus); a boastful black Republican (Wendell Pierce); and a liberal Jewish bus driver (Richard Belzer). In short, they represent a range of stereotypes. Just as the march itself has two, very different purposes, each of these men is torn between shame and regret and pride and hope. In the dialogue of what is essentially a one-set play written by Reggie Rock Bythewood, a television writer and producer and also one of the film's financial backers, the men provoke and challenge one another over the many issues that divide them.

The film, distributed by Columbia Pictures, has classic Spike Lee trademarks, such as a sure-fire Michael Jackson hit song played over a distinctive opening credit sequence, a memorable soundtrack featuring the voices of Curtis Mayfield, Stevie Wonder, and the Neville Brothers, among others, and an overall sense of uplift in spite of its confrontational tone. There are some glowing references to Louis Farrakhan, but he is not depicted; and there are only a few glimpses of the actual Million Man March. The point of the film is to convey the issues that led to the march, and Lee does that in a lively, vigorous way.

Critics hailed the acting, as well as the film's music. Janet Maslin of the *New York Times* wrote, "The film sustains the mood of gentle fellowship even when it nominally turns confrontational. Hidden amid its ideological debates there's even a musical dying to get out."[6] David Denby of *New York* magazine noted the film's "blues-anthem emotional urgency." Denby went on to say, "This gabby movie has speed and rhythm and variety. It is not a work of art but could only have been made by an artist. Get on the bus: you'll feel better at the end of the ride."[7]

Spike Lee was very proud of the film. It may have been modest, but it continued the upward trajectory of his career as a filmmaker with a striking style and an uncompromising and outspoken view of society and as an artist creating on film a world that is true to the many-faceted lives of African America, where characters and their motivations are as varied as those of other ethnic groups, where there are no easy answers.

A man of few words in conversation. Spike Lee has many conversations on film yet to create. He will continue to make films—but only on his own terms. As he told a group of students at Fisk University in April 1996, "As we move toward the millennium, the year 2000, the most powerful nations are not those that have nuclear bombs, but those that control the media. That's where the battle is being fought, that is how you control people's minds."[8]

Notes

CHAPTER 1. LITTLE GUY

1. Quoted in Gerri Hirshey, "Spike's Peak," *Vanity Fair*, June 1991, p. 88.
2. Quoted in Elvis Mitchell, "Playboy Interview: Spike Lee," *Playboy*, July 1991, p. 54.
3. Quoted in Barbara Grizzuti Harrison, "Spike Lee Strikes a Pose Behind Malcolm," *Esquire*, October 1992, pp. 132–40.
4. Quoted in Mitchell, "Playboy Interview," p. 62.
5. Hirshey, "Spike's Peak," p. 88.
6. Quoted in Mitchell, "Playboy Interview," p. 62.
7. Ibid.
8. Spike Lee et al., *Five for Five: The Films of Spike Lee* (New York: Stewart, Tabori, and Chang, 1991), p. 12.
9. Quoted in Mitchell, "Playboy Interview," 63–64.

CHAPTER 2. COLLEGE MAN

1. Quoted in Stuart Mieher, "Spike Lee's Gotta Have It," *New York Times Magazine*, August 9, 1987, p. 39.

2. Lee et al., *Five for Five*, p. 13.

3. Quoted in Hirshey, "Spike's Peak," p. 88.

4. Ibid.

5. Quoted in Harrison, "Spike Lee Strikes a Pose," p. 137.

6. Quoted in Hirshey, "Spike's Peak," p. 88.

CHAPTER 3. INDEPENDENT FILMMAKER

1. Quoted in Mieher, "Spike Lee's Gotta Have It," p. 39.

2. Lee, et al., *Five for Five*, p. 13.

3. Quoted in David Frechette, "Spike Lee's Declaration of Independence," *Black Enterprise*, December 1986, p. 56.

4. Terry McMillan, "Thoughts on *She's Gotta Have It*," in Lee et al., *Five for Five*, p. 27.

5. Ralph Novak and Peter Travers, eds., *People Weekly Magazine Guide to Movies on Video* (New York: Collier Books, 1987), p. 321.

CHAPTER 4. MUSICAL MAKER

1. Quoted in Mieher, "Spike Lee's Gotta Have It," p. 41.

2. Ibid.

3. Spike Lee with Lisa Jones, *Do the Right Thing* (New York: Simon and Schuster, 1989), p. 49.

4. Quoted in Elvis Mitchell, "A for Effort," *Rolling Stone*, July 13–17, 1989, p. 107.

CHAPTER 5. SPIKE LEE DOES THE RIGHT THING

1. Lee, *Do the Right Thing*, p. 99.

2. Quoted in "Movies," *Vogue*, July 1989, p. 75.

3. Jack Kroll, "How Hot Is Too Hot?" and David Ansen, "Searing, Nervy and Very Honest," *Newsweek*, July 3, 1989, pp. 64–65.
4. Quoted in Hirshey, "Spike's Peak," p. 88.
5. Quoted in "Movies," p. 77.

CHAPTER 6. JAZZ AND ROMANCE

1. Spike Lee with Lisa Jones, *Mo' Better Blues* (New York: Simon and Schuster, 1990), p. 39.
2. Quoted in Thulani Davis, "Denzel in the Swing," *American Film*, August 1990, p. 29.
3. Ibid.
4. Quoted in Lynn Norment, "Backstage with Spike Lee and the Cast," *Ebony*, September 1990, p. 76.
5. Quoted in Hirshey, "Spike's Peak," p. 84.
6. Quoted in Nick Ravo, "Ernest Dickerson Would Rather Be Called Director," *New York Times*, April 18, 1993, p. 19.
7. Armond White, "Amiri Baraka and Spike Lee Go Tit for Tat," *City Sun*, June 5–11, 1991, p. 15.
8. Richard Corliss, "Boyz of New Black City," *Time*, June 17, 1991, p. 64.
9. Ibid.

CHAPTER 7. SPIKE LEE'S HOME RUN

1. Quoted in Jay Carr, "Spike Lee and Malcolm X: Icons of Black Activism," *Miami Herald*, November 15, 1992, p. 2I.
2. Quoted in Sheila Rule, "Malcolm X: The Facts, the Fictions, the Film," *New York Times*, November 15, 1992, p. 23.
3. Quoted in David Ansen, "From Sinner to Martyr: A Man of Many Faces," *Newsweek*, November 16, 1992, p. 72.

4. Vincent Canby, " 'Malcolm X' as Complex as Its Subject," *New York Times*, November 18, 1992, p. C23.

5. Julie Salamon, "Film: Spike Lee's View of Malcolm X," *Wall Street Journal*, November 19, 1992, p. A11.

6. Quoted in David Denby, "Spike Lee Vows to Do the Right Thing with an Epic Malcolm X," *New York*, September 14, 1992, p. 84.

CHAPTER 8. TEN-YEAR VETERAN, WITH THE SCARS TO PROVE IT

1. Quoted in "Spike Lee" segment on *60 Minutes*, April 7, 1996.

2. Quoted in David Bradley, "Spike Lee's Inferno, The Drug Underworld," *New York Times*, September 10, 1995, p. 29.

3. Quoted in Bernard Weinraub, "Black Film Makers Are Looking Beyond Ghetto Violence," *New York Times*, September 11, 1995, p. C11.

4. Quoted in Bruce Kirkland, "No Cannes Do, Director Says: Spike Lee Rants Against Film Awards," *Toronto Sun*, May 12, 1996, p. 1.

5. Quoted in John Horn, "Spike Lee Is at a Film Career Crossroads," Associated Press, April 2, 1996, no page.

6. Janet Maslin, "An Anniversary Tribute to the Million Man March," New York Times, October 16, 1996, p. C11.

7. David Denby, "Ticket to Ride," New York, October 21, 1996, p. 53.

8. Quoted in "Spike Lee Talks About Control," Associated Press, April 10, 1996, no page.

Selected Bibliography

Bernotas, Bob. *Spike Lee: Filmmaker*. Hillside, N.J.: Enslow Publishers, 1993.

Lee, Spike. *Spike Lee's She's Gotta Have It: Inside Guerrilla Filmmaking*. New York: Simon and Schuster, 1987.

Lee, Spike, with Lisa Jones. *Do the Right Thing*. New York: Simon and Schuster, 1989.

———. *Mo' Better Blues*. New York: Simon and Schuster, 1990.

Lee, Spike, et al. *Five for Five: The Films of Spike Lee*. New York: Stewart, Tabori, and Chang, 1991.

Novak, Ralph, and Peter Travers, eds. *People Weekly Magazine Guide to Movies on Video*. New York: Collier Books, 1987.

Patterson, Alex. *Spike Lee*. New York: Avon Books, 1992.

Index

Index

Index

Index

Index

Index